The Inconjunct:

Natal and Transiting Aspects

Frances Sakoian
and
Louis Acker

ISBN-10: 0-86690-627-4
ISBN-13: 978-0-86690-627-2

Cover Design: Jack Cipolla

Published by:
American Federation of Astrologers, Inc.
6535 S. Rural Road
Tempe, AZ 85283

www.astrologers.com

Printed in the United States of America

Contents

Part One

The Natal Inconjunct

1

The Natal Inconjunct

An inconjunct is an aspect of 150°, and two planets that form this aspect will have approximately the same degree—five signs apart, or 30° more than a trine and 30° less than an opposition. For example, Aries is inconjunct Scorpio, Taurus is inconjunct Sagittarius, Gemini is inconjunct Capricorn, etc. The inconjunct, by its very nature, always involves elements that are incompatible, such as fire and water or fire and earth.

Because the natural zodiac is used to define the basic sign and planetary rulership of aspects, the inconjunct has a sixth house-Virgo-Mercury connotation, and an eighth house-Scorpio-Mars-Uranus-Pluto connotation. For this reason, the inconjunct aspect deals with karmic situations related to the use of desire, and is also connected with the creative thinking processes.

We must bear in mind that the mind is always creating something, whether the product is constructive or destructive. The process and the thought created are dependent upon the focus of the will or the attention. The focus of the attention, which is chosen from instant to instant, creates a mental blueprint into which the desire energy, represented by Mars, is focused. This desire impetus brings about action that causes the materialization of thought in situations and circumstances on the practical, material level of ex-

3

perience. This final manifestation is entirely linked to the nature of the original mental blueprint.

In this respect, Mercury acts as a lens or focusing device between the spiritual will or the self-conscious direction of attention represented by the Sun exalted in Aries. Pluto, co-ruler of Aries and Scorpio, which is exalted in Sun-ruled Leo, involves the desire principle represented by Mars as ruler of Aries and Scorpio.

Only through careful, conscious examination of the thinking process can an individual know if a chosen thought will later attract desire and bring about favorable or unfavorable circumstances resulting from actions taken. Difficult situations that are created are often a direct product of undisciplined thinking and this is the essence of the inconjunct aspect.

Free will exists only in the realm of our conscious choice of the subject of our mental attention and the decision concerning what thoughts we will entertain. The rest of the process—the manifestation of these thoughts—is an automatic process of natural law.

Most people do not realize what they have set into motion by the thoughts they entertain, until they are confronted with the material circumstances which the thought created. Instead, they consider themselves to be the victims of conditions over which they have no control.

In actuality, however, through their unconscious and unwise use of thought-power, they have set in motion the causes that brought about the resulting circumstances.

It is obvious that no task can be done well if the attention is not on the work at hand at the time that the work is being done. Most mistakes are made because people allow their attention to wander to something extraneous to the job at hand. The end result of this, of course, is inefficiency and wasted effort. Therefore, to resolve problems involving the quincunx aspect, it is necessary to carefully examine the mental habit patterns and emotional, desire patterns which can obstruct impartial, objective thinking.

One of the difficulties with the inconjunct is that its influence spans a broad range of levels of psychic and material attributes. It is important to note that the highest level of spiritual will in astrology involves the Sun and Pluto. People contain within their make-up what metaphysicians call subtle bodies or interacting and interpenetrating fields that are constructed of different vibratory rates of energy. For instance, the mental body is the strata of energy in people on which memory patterns are recorded and thought patterns are developed and communicated to the emotional nature. This is then passed to the desire body and then on to the etheric or vitality body, which then impresses the pattern on the nervous system of the body.

The processes of the mental body are closely linked with the planet Mercury, which rules the sign Virgo and the sixth house. This is the place in the horoscope in which thought is put into concrete manifestation through work, or its influence is felt in physical health.

Mars, which is also linked with the quincunx aspect through the sign Scorpio, is closely related to the functions of desire or the desire body which is also called the astral body. This is the strata of energy on which man's emotional function takes place.

According to these references to the various bodies and their relationship to specific planets and signs involved in the inconjunct aspect, we are aware that a wide range of levels that constitute one's expression are covered. Difficulties arise when widely divergent levels are at cross purposes, and if these difficulties are to be avoided, a conscious and harmonious interplay is required on all levels. The inconjunct aspect often manifests as a "time bind," causing situations in which many demands are made at once—situations with which the individual is unable to cope.

Time is the major factor needed to solve these problems, and it does no good to try to force matters to conclusion. The lesson involves conscientious attention to responsibilities. When this occurs in other people involved in the situation, it is merely a reflection of what was probably lacking at one time in the individual who is experiencing the difficulty. Recognition of the character attributes that need improvement in order to avoid similar situations in the future is finally brought to the consciousness of the individual.

Because of the time-lag between thought and physical manifestation implied in such a broad span of levels of consciousness, the inconjunct can manifest as frustration due to being mentally ahead of the reality of practical circumstances, or it can manifest as being mentally or emotionally out of touch with practical responsibilities. In such cases, the solution is patience, detached objectivity, and attention to detail. Any attempt to force or evade the issue only aggravates the problem.

In short, the inconjunct is an object lesson in the consequences of incorrect thought, desire, and action. One is made aware of what is needed in terms of efficiency, correct conduct, and effective attention to tasks in order to solve the situation.

2

Natal Sun

Inconjuncts involving the Sun in the natal chart can manifest in the following ways:

- Difficulties relating to health and vitality.
- Obstacles in the way of achieving personal goals and ambitions.
- Egotism and pride may stand in the way of successful relationships with coworkers, employers, and employees, or the individual may be forced to work with people who have a similar temperament.
- Danger involving speculation, joint resources, taxes, and insurance. One may be caught up in events pertaining to these matters and be helpless to do anything to alleviate the situation. There is often a lack of willpower pertaining to these matters.
- Difficulties with children and their health.

Sun Inconjunct Moon

The Sun, the giver of life and vitality, inconjunct the Moon, ruler of the etheric body, indicates problems with health and vitality due to an incorrect flow of pranic or solar forces through the body. This is likely to manifest as an emotional, ill-at-ease feeling or malaise which constantly irritates the person from a level just below conscious awareness.

There is a need to regenerate the interaction between the emotional responses and the conscious will through intelligently directed, constructive work. This, in return, will give the individual a feeling of self-assurance and worth that will contribute to psychological stability.

The above-mentioned difficulties are apt to influence domestic and family relations. It is also likely to involve one's ability to get along with the opposite sex, especially in romantic situations.

Sun Inconjunct Mars

This aspect can cause great emotional excitement and irritability, often resulting in conflict between the will and the desire nature. There can be irritation because of the laziness and inefficiency of others, or sometimes it is caused by the individual's own lack of ability to efficiently and meaningfully direct the energies.

The solution to this problem can be found in carefully thinking out the situation beforehand and allowing calmness and patience to prevail. Anger and resentment can cause health problems, often manifesting as fevers and inflammations of various kinds, especially if the Sun or Mars is in a fire sign.

This individual must learn to consider the rights and needs of others concerning joint resources and coworkers.

There can also be danger of accidental injury because of rashness and impulsiveness. Care should be taken in exercising adequate safety precautions, especially if the activity requires the use of machinery or sharp tools.

Sun Inconjunct Jupiter

With this quincunx, there is a tendency to overextend oneself by taking on too many responsibilities. This result from overlooking all the details involved in carrying out a promise or goal. Consequently, the individual either incurs disfavor by letting people down, or becomes overworked.

Health problems can arise through overindulgence in food, alcohol, and sweets.

There can be litigation and difficulties concerning taxes, insurance, inheritance, alimony, and corporate resources.

Educational difficulties can arise if the individual pursues advanced fields of study without first laying the groundwork and learning the fundamentals.

These individuals can advance spiritually by pursuing practical work, as this aspect demands effort and constructive action in order to achieve significant gains.

Sun Inconjunct Saturn

This aspect can indicate ill health because of negative, self-limiting attitudes, fearfulness, and overwork. Sometimes these people are so engrossed in the details of their work that they lose the overall perspective of the relative value of what they are doing.

There can be difficulties in dealing with superiors or inferiors who are involved in their work, and they may even embrace the concept that they are the only ones who know how to efficiently organize their own work. This self-righteous attitude can cause ill will among coworkers or those in authority. As a result, they are apt to feel unappreciated, which further compounds the difficulty.

These people can be dedicated workers; however, they are apt to feel sorry for themselves and neglect to look for new or different ways of doing things. They must learn to be more receptive to innovation and the creative qualities in others. When frustrated, it is because of their own constrictive, negative, and crystallized attitudes.

Sun Inconjunct Uranus

This inconjunct can cause instability concerning work and health. Often there is a tendency to act without sufficient knowledge so that the chances of success are jeopardized. These people often lack continuity of purpose in their occupation, and therefore have difficulty adjusting to routine work and responsibilities.

In relationships with coworkers and superiors, there can be a know-it-all attitude, which can cause resentment in others.

Safety precautions should be strictly observed when working with electricity, explosives, tools, and mechanical devices.

If these people can learn to overcome these difficulties, they can utilize their resourcefulness and originality by finding new ways to solve problems and then carry out the necessary actions.

The need to remake friends without first remaking themselves can result in unpopularity. On the other hand, however, friends may try to remake these individuals.

Unpredictable circumstances can arise involving conditions surrounding employment, coworkers, employees, joint finances, taxes, insurance, and inheritance.

These individuals are apt to be interested in the occult forces of nature, especially those that govern life after death.

Sun Inconjunct Neptune

These individuals are often prone to illnesses that are difficult to diagnose. These physical disorders are often psychosomatic or caused by interference from unwholesome psychic forces.

Extreme care must be taken in the use of drugs and medication because these people can be easily poisoned by foreign matter. Overindulgence in alcohol can also have an adverse effect.

Sometimes ill health can result in long periods of incarceration in hospitals or other institutions.

These people often have difficulties holding a job because of a tendency to drift or to be unreliable. They may work in a large institution, and may have the feeling that coworkers, other employees or the boss are undermining them in some way. This can, however, be the result of their own overly active imagination.

In the case of a hard-working, intelligent, reliable person, this aspect can result in a situation in which these people are is forced to witness and cope with chaotic, inefficient, and undisciplined situations concerning work.

Mysterious and difficult circumstances can come about through taxes, insurance, inheritance and joint finances. Sometimes there can be treachery concerning corporate money or joint finances.

There often is an interest in or the ability to communicate with spirits.

Sun Inconjunct Pluto

Ths inconjunct gives a strong will and a sound determination concerning work, but the work can involve matters of great danger and seriousness, including those of life and death.

Investigators of life after death, reincarnation, and other occult forces are apt to have this aspect.

Often there is a strong desire to constantly improve the methods used in work, but obstacles usually stand in their way. Someone in authority may constantly putting these people under pressure to improve their work.

This work can involve advanced technological research on the frontiers of scientific knowledge, but there can be frustration because of financial difficulties and limitations. Often the work is carried on in secret or seclusion.

There are apt to be difficulties concerning the affairs of the dead, taxes and insurance.

3

Natal Moon

Inconjuncts involving the Moon in the natal chart can manifest in the following ways:

- Health difficulties caused by indigestion and improper dietary habits.
- Difficulties related to emotional equilibrium.
- Emotional and family problems can stand in the way of their work and good relationships on the job. They may be burdened by the responsibility of taking care of the health or the affairs of a family member who has died or is chronically ill.
- Disputes with other family members over inheritance, including conditions beyond their control. Similar difficulties may arise over taxes, insurance, the home, and family property.
- Conditions stemming from the past, as well as dealings with the public, can also results in difficulties.

Moon Inconjunct Mercury

This inconjunct indicates health problems caused by improper dietary habits, digestion, or hygiene. At times, the inadequate diet is caused by an unavailability of suitable food while traveling or visiting unfamiliar places. Emotional nervousness can also cause digestive upsets.

These individuals are apt to have difficulty in their work and in relationships with coworkers, other employees, or employers because of their indiscriminate talking about trivial, inconsequential matters. Often they may say the wrong thing at the wrong time to the wrong people. These individuals also have difficulty keeping secrets because of the eighth-house connotation of the inconjunct aspect.

Nervousness and restlessness can also contribute to their inefficiency at work.

There can also be difficulties communicating with women, or these people may find themselves in situations in which women are constantly talking and coming and going to the point of annoyance.

Moon Inconjunct Venus

This aspect can indicate ill health that occurs because of overindulgence in sweets and other foods eaten to please rather than to fulfill nutritional needs.

Ill health can also be the result of indiscriminate overindulgence in sexual activities. Sex is related to Venus, which represents emotional attraction, while the inconjunct deals with Scorpio and the eighth house.

Periods of ill health may interfere with romance, socializing, and emotional well-being.

Artistic judgment concerning home furnishings and dress may lack good taste. On the other hand, their work may involve such things as interior design or dressmaking.

Although these individuals are apt to be style-conscious, the quality of their judgment will depend on the rest of the horoscope. Concern over these matters may cause aggravation because of the need to continually modify and improve their decor and clothing.

Moon Inconjunct Mars

This can indicate ill health and accidents as a result of irritability and anger issues. This state of anger and emotional agitation is often caused by inharmonious relations with people at work or in the domestic environment. And a lack of emotional control can divert the native's attention from the job at hand, thus increasing the chance for accidents at home or in the workplace.

It's also possible that these people can be forced to deal with ill-tempered people in the family or work environment.

These difficulties, however, are often caused by their own lack of emotional control and inability to remain calm under stressful circumstances. Many of these difficulties can be avoided if they cultivate an attitude of detachment and impersonal involvement in situations that directly involve them.

These people should be especially careful when using machinery or other potentially dangerous equipment and tools. Difficulties can be avoided if cautionary measures are followed.

Moon Inconjunct Jupiter

This aspect can indicate health concerns because of overindulgence in rich foods.

Job and career may involve religious institutions or employment in higher education.

These people are apt to cause themselves difficulties either by taking on more responsibilities than they can handle or by overworking or failing to meet commitments. They may even upset their own equilibrium by becoming involved with others who have overextended their resources.

It's also possible these people will need to handle work that other people have left unfinished or that was improperly executed. This can result in emotional upset.

Legal complications or religious attitudes of family members can interfere with their work and happiness. At times, family problems, in general, can interfere with work, health, or both.

There can also be legal difficulties concerning land, property, joint finances, and inheritance.

Because of their exuberant need to do something of major consequence, these people often cause themselves difficulties. They need to consider all the details required to complete any task before beginning it, as well as while working on it.

Moon Inconjunct Saturn

This inconjunct increases the possibility for health problems caused by depression and emotional conditions. Ill health can also result from sluggish digestion or eating food that is too heavy for the system to handle.

These people are often overworked, or feel they are. The cause is often a self-limiting attitude that overlooks other opportunities and faster, more efficient ways of doing things.

Sometimes these people are disliked in the family and workplace because of a dour attitude, thus cutting them off from the contact they need for emotional happiness and personal advancement. They may also be victims of people in the domestic or work environment who have a limiting and negative emotional outlook. Some are burdened by the need to care for a sick or elderly family member.

All of the above can cause a sense of martyrdom that others find difficult. These people need to develop optimism and a fresh outlook, combined with a willingness to try new avenues of expression in order to overcome their sense of futility and limitation.

Moon Inconjunct Uranus

This inconjunct can cause difficulties through unreliability and eccentric emotional behavior at work or in the home. Ultimately, this can lead to employment difficulties because of a reputation for undependability and an unwillingness to follow orders and the established routine.

These people can antagonize employers and coworkers because of a know-it-all attitude and refusing to consider the advice of those who are wiser, better educated, or more experienced. This aspect can make it difficult for these people to function harmoniously in a group effort. Some become involved in labor disputes and protests that upset work conditions and home life.

Extremes of emotion can cause ill health because of a strain on the nervous system which, in turn, affects the digestion.

Friends and family are likely to dislike and be confused by their erratic behavior. On the positive side, however, they can devise ingenious work methods that increase efficiency. Also positive is the ability to make friends through work and to become involved in group activities of a humanitarian or charitable nature.

Moon Inconjunct Neptune

This can indicate health difficulties because of overindulgence in alcohol, drugs, or food. The body is extremely sensitive to foreign matter; therefore, processed foods should be avoided.

Confusion in domestic relationships can cause emotional stress that interferes with work and results in health problems.

These people may have job difficulties related to laziness, indolence, and confusion concerning the practical details of what is required of them. It's also possible they may be a victim of lazy or irresponsible people in the workplace or domestic environment.

Some of these people work in hospitals, institutions, or other large organizations where they are one of the masses.

Should other astrological factors concur, mental or physical health can create the need for long-term hospitalization. Poor care, improper drugs, careless personnel, and an inadequate diet are possible during this institutionalization.

Moon Inconjunct Pluto

This inconjunct can indicate difficulties in work or health as a result of severe emotional reactions and uncompromising attitudes. In extreme cases, work-related accidents can be fatal.

These people or others in the domestic environment may constantly remodel, change, or improve the home to the point where these activities become a source of irritation.

The home can be damaged or destroyed by natural disasters such as earthquakes, tornadoes, and hurricanes, or as a result of social upheaval, and these people can be strongly affected by the death or illness of family members.

There can also be conflict with family members, property, inheritance, and joint finances, all of which can affect the health.

These people may be overly concerned with changing or improving the emotional behavior of those in the domestic or work environment, or they may be a victim of such influences.

4

Natal Mercury

Inconjuncts involving Mercury in the natal chart can manifest in the following ways:

- Possible health problems related to nervousness and digestion, especially those related to the intestines.
- Too many diverse responsibilities that impede the effective execution of work, and this, in turn, affects the health.
- Problems related to effective communication with coworkers, other employees, and the employer that interfere with job success. Lack of education can thwart career ambitions and make it difficult to find a suitable job.
- Financial difficulties related to fraudulent or otherwise ill-considered contracts involving insurance, inheritance, taxes, or corporate or business matters.

Mercury Inconjunct Mars

This aspect indicates an inclination for irritability, which can wear on the nerves, thus causing these people to experience ill health because of mental tension. Nervous disorders and a critical temperament are possible.

An irritable temperament can lead to difficult relationships with employers and coworkers. Although these people have ideas that can improve the work environment, they often lack the tact and diplomacy needed to present them. Consequently, they irritate others in the workplace.

These people should avoid a know-it-all attitude, and learn to listen to others. Then, they can attain great happiness, stability, and efficiency in work, especially when a calm, observant demeanor is cultivated and unnecessary criticism of others is curbed.

There is apt to be a conflict between desire and reason, which can cause additional problems. These people need to carefully evaluate their desires and choose only those that are worthwhile. Then they must decide if they want to invest the mental and physical energy required to realize them.

Impatience is a difficulty inherent in this aspect. If carried too far, it can lead to accidents involving the hands and fingers. Careful attention to work and safety precautions are a must.

These people are likely to worry about taxes, insurance, inheritance, joint resources, and divorce-related financial matters.

Mercury Inconjunct Jupiter

This Mercury-Jupiter aspect tends to bring difficulties related to jobs and responsibilities that are too much to handle without overwork. Essential details are neglected. They should learn to master small tasks and skills before attempting to do larger projects.

They will often look far afield for new things to do while neglecting that which is in front of them. Others find their platitudes and meaningless generalizations annoying, especially those who are focused on their own work.

But these people can also be victimized by well-intentioned but inefficient employees, employers, and coworkers. Accidents can occur and their health can be negatively affected by indiscretion in driving, disorganization, and a lack of hygiene in the environment.

Dietary habits are not always sensible, and a poor diet can harm the nervous system and liver.

These people love to suggest that others perform work and services that will help the larger social order, while they neglect their own work. This tendency comes from a desire to deal with large philosophical concepts without having the patience to examine the practical details involved in these endeavors.

Often there is great concern for improving the lot of humanity in faraway places, but at the same time these people will neglect their own immediate surroundings.

Mercury Inconjunct Saturn

This inconjunct is associated with people who are hard working and exacting, but who experience difficulties because of a negative and narrow outlook concerning work and health. In other words, they tend to get themselves in a rut and are often unwilling to try new ways of doing things.

They can be thwarted in their work and career because of a lack of educational opportunities, and for this reason be forced to do monotonous tasks with insufficient recognition for their labors. A critical or jealous attitude can be the result, and this can cause poor relationships with coworkers, employers, and other employees. They generally do not feel loved or appreciated. Occasionally, these people are hampered by delays in vital communication in the workplace.

Negative mental attitudes combined with overwork often bring about conditions of chronic ill health or merely a sense of weariness. This state of mind can lead to rheumatic or respiratory disorders. Periods of ill health can interfere with their ability to work and maintain financial security.

These people may find themselves in positions where they are forced to care for the ill or elderly, which in turn interferes with their own life progress.

At times they can be in a position that forces them to depend upon people who are slow, inefficient, or narrow-minded.

Mercury Inconjunct Uranus

This inconjunct may create problems in work and health because of the inability to adjust to routine responsibilities. They often have good ideas, but there is a lack of discipline to take action on them.

These people have a tendency to irritate those with whom they work because of a know-it-all attitude. They can antagonize employers and coworkers because of their unreliability and desire to initiate change merely for the sake of change.

Irregular living and working habits can result in nervous disorders as well as a disorderly environment. Nervous disorders can result, causing them to be restless and irritable. These people should therefore develop the ability to listen to those who are more experienced, and should cultivate patience and steadiness regarding education and work. They also should avoid promoting unqualified friends as potential employees.

At times these people are exposed to people who display similar negative qualities, and they experience the same kind of difficulties as a result. Associations with these kinds of people can upset them greatly.

Mercury Inconjunct Neptune

This inconjunct may indicate difficulties caused by laziness, daydreaming, and unreliability in the work environment. It may also bring about difficulties in health because of an improper diet, excessive drinking or drug abuse.

Sometimes psychological based illness or ill health can cause hospitalization or incarceration, and the subsequent inability to work. In short, these people have a hard time facing the responsibility of a practical, realistic approach to life.

Often these people are prone to psychosomatic ailments, or there may be physical problems that are difficult to diagnose.

These people have a tendency to avoid facing responsibilities and duties, which causes resentment at work. A tendency for escapism can make them dependent upon those who are more disciplined, including persuading them to help. Some of these people drift from job to job, accomplishing little, and even good ideas go nowhere because of the lack of follow-through. However, in some cases, these people may be quite capable but hampered by others who display these traits.

This aspect can also indicate deceit or an inability to communicate in areas regarding work, health, and practical responsibilities.

Mercury Inconjunct Pluto

People with this aspect may have difficulties in the areas of work and health because of an authoritative, overbearing attitude. Intellectual arrogance can cause ill will with coworkers and employers.

These people constantly try to improve the status quo of their work situation to the point at which it generates nervousness and apprehension in coworkers. They may themselves be subjected to employers and coworkers who are exacting and critical, constantly demanding improvement in work methods and performance.

They are often forced to work within conditions that are dangerous or hazardous to life and health. For example, someone whose work involves high explosives could have this aspect, and in such a case a mistake could result in an accident. Or, the work life could involve a high level of secrecy, and resulting dire consequences if the information were to be divulged.

Ill health and nervous disorders can be caused by irritability and caustic speech.

5

Natal Venus

Inconjuncts involving Venus in the natal chart can manifest in the following ways:

- A tendency for health problems as a result of sexual relations.
- Excessive socializing can affect relationships and productivity.
- Marriage and other partnerships, as well as the public image, may cause difficulties that affect job matters and consequently the health.
- The use of charm or personal friendship to acquire employment for which they are not qualified, thus leading to embarrassment and poor relationships. They may be listless and languid workers, or victimized by others who are lazy or indifferent.
- Financial difficulties as a result of improperly defined duties and responsibilities concerning joint resources, taxes, insurance, inheritance, and funds belonging to other people. Financial challenges can also arise as a result of divorce, and there may be a tendency to squander other people's money or to stand helplessly by while others squander do the same.

Venus Inconjunct Mars

This combination indicates possible difficulties in personal relationships, which can then have an adverse effect on work and health. The wrong kind of social and sexual interaction may lead to illness, which in turn can interfere with the daily work schedule and responsibilities.

Romantic involvement with other employees, coworkers, or employers can interfere with the job responsibilities and security, but at the same time, professional responsibilities can interfere with romance, marriage, and social life.

At work, these people can alternate between intense cooperation and stubborn insistence that generates from the need to do things their own way, thus confusing themselves and especially bosses and coworkers. There can be disagreements concerning the relationship between personal resources and family or business resources.

Sometimes these people are drawn into the drama of those around them—people who do not know how to regulate their social and romantic behavior during work hours. This can interfere with productivity and physical and mental well-being.

Venus Inconjunct Jupiter

This inconjunct indicates potential for stressful situations related to the need for personal, emotional satisfaction and those derived from impersonal, social ideals and purposes. This can manifest as a conflict between the native's personal, sexual, and romantic desires and moral attitudes that were ingrained through education and religious training.

Overindulgence in food, pleasure, luxury, and socializing may interfere with work and learning, and also cause ill health due to excessive weight, a poor diet, or an excessive indulgence.

Socializing at work with other employees, coworkers, or employers may interfere with getting the job done, or these people can be hampered by those around them who would rather socialize than accomplish their appointed tasks.

Venus Inconjunct Saturn

These people may have work and health difficulties related to depression and low self-confidence. Their lack of interaction on a social level with other employees, coworkers, and employers can interfere with career advancement. Professional responsibilities may also interfere with social and romantic opportunities, as can ill health or having to care for those who are ill can also interfere with the native's social, professional, and romantic opportunities.

There are apt to be periods of unemployment that may cause financial hardship. Or, on the other hand, work responsibilities may keep these people from enjoying what they have earned. In any event, there is apt to be an imbalance between work and pleasure, and they are unlikely to enjoy their work either because of an inappropriate attitude or because the work itself has an abundance of unpleasant drudgery associated with it.

Often these people are oppressed by others who are older and more established in that there is little opportunity for advancement. However, there can be a lack of opportunity because of their own negative, personal attitudes and lack of creative innovations. This often manifests in a crystallized, institutionalized power structure that does not recognize individual merit.

Venus Inconjunct Uranus

This inconjunct creates an ongoing need for social and emotional excitement that can interfere with reliability and stability in the performance of ordinary tasks and responsibilities.

As with the Venus-Jupiter inconjunct, too much social activity while on the job can interfere with productivity. Consequently, there can be a lack of stability in employment, which then interferes with financial and personal stability. This can, in turn, cause health problems due to inappropriate living situations. (Other factors in the horoscope should bear this out.) Indiscriminate sexual activities can also lead to health problems, or they may interfere with stability in marriage or other personal relationships.

If these people do not have these personal challenges, they may be hampered by friends, coworkers, other employees, employers, or partners who do. In some cases, they may try to bring friends into the workplace who are not properly qualified or disciplined enough to handle the responsibilities. This, in turn, affects their reputation, productivity, and well-being.

Venus Inconjunct Neptune

This inconjunct may indicate an impractical concern with pleasures and amusements that do not contribute to practical daily life and overall well-being. In some cases this may lead to an escapist tendency that causes these people to seek exotic pleasures and unsuitable social contacts as a means to avoid routine, practical responsibilities.

As with Venus inconjunct Mars and Venus inconjunct Uranus, indiscriminate sexual activity may cause health problems and interfere with work or in some way create a financial strain.

At times, this aspect may indicate secret romances or partnerships that impact health and personal resources. On the other hand, these people may be a victim of a deceptive partner who engages in such activities.

An escapist tendency can manifest as alcoholism or drug abuse, which can lead to illness and unreliability concerning work and career. For this to be a severe problem, however, look to other aspects in the chart for confirmation.

These people can be influenced in a negative way through their association with people who interfere with the performance of necessary responsibilities. These people may be employers, other employees, coworkers, partners, or social contacts.

Venus Inconjunct Pluto

Venus inconjunct Pluto is similar to Venus inconjunct Mars or Uranus, except that the interactions tend to be of a more subtle and secretive nature.

These people may suffer emotionally because of the ill health or the death of a loved one, which may in turn interfere with their health or opportunities for job progress.

They can make become unpopular if they constantly try to reform the social habits and attitudes of those with whom they're associated through work, partnership, or marriage, and may themselves be subjected to such treatment on the part of others.

Their romantic and sexual activities and other social indulgences are likely to interfere with their financial stability and job performance. Unwise sexual indulgence may cause health problems.

In some cases, these people may be required to participate in social activities they do not enjoy or approve of in order to advance their careers.

6

Natal Mars

Inconjuncts involving Mars in the natal chart can manifest in the following ways:

- Work and health may suffer because of rash actions and decisions, impulsiveness, impatience, and an inability to control the temper.
- Injuries and accidents may occur at work as a result of their own or coworkers' lack of attention to safety precautions.
- Potential for difficult predicaments and arguments with coworkers, other employees, and employers, or that they may be subjected to people in th workplace who are combative and disagreeable.
- Insurance, taxes, corporate money, and inheritance are likely to be sources of difficulty.

Mars Inconjunct Jupiter

This inconjunct indicates an overzealous attitude toward work and goals. As a result, these people often bites off more than they can chew, and thus fall short of their mark or do an inadequate job because of their failure to see all of the details.

Stress can come into their life as a result of involvement in military, religious, or political endeavors that are not properly defined or planned.

At times, unrealistic goals can be set in education or religious activities. These people must remember that before they can save the world, they must first become the best they can be.

Their desire to crusade for causes may antagonize those for whom they advocate their ideals, or they may be subjected to the same treatment from others.

An arrogant attitude toward coworkers, other employees, and employers may result in resentment that can jeopardize job security. In addition, these people may be subjected to the influence of people who have these character defects.

Mars Inconjunct Saturn

People with this inconjunct have a disciplined, hard-working attitude toward life in general and employment in particular. Despite their discipline, however, they are likely to experience job difficulties because of their rigid attitudes and inability to cooperate with others.

They can antagonize other employees, coworkers, and employers by being exceedingly exacting and uncompromising in their demands.

Their personal initiative may be thwarted by crystallized, established rules and institutions, or they may impose rigid procedures on those with whom they work.

Another way this inconjunct can manifest is in the form of irritation when others attempt to bring innovative ideas and methods into the established way of doing things.

Unsafe conditions under which they work can result in accidents that affect their health and ability to work. This can work slowly through environmental pollution factors, in addition to sudden accidents. Employment may require hard physical labor involving machinery, dirty conditions, and intense noise. Ill health can be the result of overwork or too much personal responsibility.

Mars Inconjunct Uranus

This inconjunct indicates an impulsive, overly confident, or impatient attitude toward work which results in accidents, mistakes, or the antagonism of those with whom they associate in the work environment.

In extreme cases a lack of concern for safety in work can endanger life. This is because of the triple Scorpio/eighth-house emphasis, Mars, Uranus, and the nature of the inconjunct aspect itself.

In some cases, friends may influence these people to take impulsive, ill-considered actions. These rash and impulsive acts may lead to ill health, causing an inability to work.

Since these people are apt to be restless, they also have an inability to adjust to routine tasks and responsibilities, and this may cause frequent changes in employment. This tendency can eventually give them an unfavorable work reputation.

Their temperament is also likely to antagonize those with whom they work, causing a loss of friends and sometimes a loss of job. They need to cultivate patience and the ability to listen to others.

In some cases, they may be subjected to the influence of people who have the above described character traits.

Mars Inconjunct Neptune

People with this inconjunct are restless and lack discipline concerning work and practical responsibilities.

They are apt to have unrealistic ambitions regarding their goals and future achievements, especially in the career/job area.

Often this inconjunct indicates the need to work with conditions that are nebulous and ill-defined, which results in a sense of confusion and insecurity concerning their work life.

The people with whom they work are often confused about what they intend to do and how they intend to do it, thus causing feelings of disorientation and discontent.

Unhealthy desires may lead to an overindulgence in alcohol, drugs, and sex, all of which may cause unreliability, ill health, and an inability to work.

In any event, there will be some kind of activity that will undermine their health and work. Unfortunately, these people may have peculiar illnesses that are difficult to diagnose and that may slowly undermine their health and ability to work.

Mars Inconjunct Pluto

These people have an aggressive and domineering attitude regarding work and ambitions. They are likely to be bossy toward coworkers, which results in opposition and unpopularity.

The conditions of their work could be secretive or dangerous, and in extreme cases, life could be endangered or the ability to work could be impeded in some way.

This aspect may also indicate that these people are subject to those who constantly plague them to do a better job or to improve their health. On the other hand, these people may use these tactics on others, consequently resulting in unpopularity.

People whose work involves advanced forms of physics or atomic energy may have this aspect.

7

Natal Jupiter

Inconjuncts involving the Sun in the natal chart can manifest in the following ways:

- Overindulge can cause health problems. There may also be health problems or diseases contracted while traveling or while studying in an institution of higher learning.
- Concerning work, these people are either lazy or willing to take on more work than they are capable of fulfilling. This is often the result of a tendency to underestimate the amount of work that a given task requires because of insufficient attention to detail. They may be subjected to people who have the same flaws, and therefore be the ones who experience these conditions.
- Religious or cultural prejudices may be an obstacle that prevents them from finding employment. Conversely, they may harbor such prejudices against others.
- Insufficient or improper education may interfere with their success on the job.
- Legal difficulties and entanglements may cause problems with employment, labor unions, inheritance, taxes, insurance, child support, spousal maintenance, and corporate money.

Jupiter Inconjunct Saturn

Jupiter inconjunct Saturn indicates health and work problems arising out of a faulty sense of timing, and either excessive optimism or too much reserve.

Often their propensity to vacillate between extremes of behavior affect daily work, career endeavors, and dietary habits and disciplines.

These people must learn to tread a middle path between being cautious and proceeding with unrealistic expectations.

Their professional ambitions are often thwarted by an inadequate or faulty education.

The inconjunct can also indicate that these people thwart the optimism and expansion of their coworkers, other employees, employers, or partners by being too conservative. On the other hand, they may be thwarted by people or institutions that are crystallized or overly conservative.

However, their tedious and sometimes self-righteous attitudes can alienate those with whom they work. Religious prejudices and convictions may also cause difficulties concerning work as these people may impose their religious beliefs on coworkers, other employees, or employers—or vice versa. In some cases, religious prejudice may stand in the way of their career opportunities.

At times these people may be burdened by the responsibility of caring for elderly people who are ill, or they may themselves become chronically ill during the later years of life.

There can be legal problems over inheritance, taxes, insurance, or joint finances.

Jupiter Inconjunct Uranus

These people may have difficulties with health and work as a result of inappropriate optimism and ill-considered expansion. They may experience ill health as a result of excesses of various kinds.

This optimism is apt to be impractical because of insufficient attention to details and a lack of consideration of the advice of those who are more experienced.

They can save himself abundant grief by testing an idea on a small scale before trying it out on a larger scale. If this is not done, they run the risk of losing large sums of money should the venture be unsuccessful.

These people are apt to get into legal difficulties by encouraging others to invest in a project which is impractical and groundless, thus resulting in lawsuits concerning finances and investments.

They are to be considered as impractical dreamers by those who work with them, or they may be subject to coworkers, other employees, or employers who have unrealistic expectations.

Education may be directed in the pursuit of so-called higher spiritual or philosophic wisdom, but this is inadequate preparation for a practical career that enables them to take care of their physical needs.

Personal friendships can interfere with the selection of qualified people to help them in their work or health. On the other hand, they may be denied advancement because of favoritism.

There can also be litigation regarding joint money, taxes, insurance, and inheritance.

Jupiter Inconjunct Neptune

These people have illusionary attitudes and expectations concerning work and health. They often have high-sounding, spiritual sentiments about charity and service with little substance or work to back them up. At times they may feel inspired from "on high" to do certain types of work or perform a certain type of service.

They are apt to incur the disfavor of employers, other employees, or coworkers by taking too much for granted. They can be lax in their performance of duty, yet expect something for nothing. On the other hand, they may be subjected to people with such attitudes.

These people can also lose an inheritance or other money as a result of fraud, or they may squander money on an unrealistic project.

As with Jupiter inconjunct Uranus, their education is apt to be lacking in practicality.

Health and work can be affected in an adverse manner by excessive eating or drinking, or drug use.

Jupiter Inconjunct Pluto

These people cause difficulties in their work life and health by constantly moralizing and trying to reform those with whom they work. They delude themselves by thinking that such comments are "for their own good."

These are the people who are apt to aggressively try to convert coworkers, other employees, or employers to their own religious dogma. It could work the other way, however, in which case they would be subjected to such treatment.

In extreme cases, coercion might be used in order to make others conform to their beliefs, or these people may be denied the opportunity to work unless they subscribe to the standards of others.

Inappropriate or inadequate education can stand in the way of professional opportunities.

Legal difficulties may arise from inheritance, taxes, insurance, and joint finances.

These people may have a philosophic interest in life after death, occult forces, etc.

8

Natal Saturn

Inconjuncts involving Saturn in the natal chart can manifest in the following ways:

- Health problems caused by depression and a lack of vitality. In turn, these can manifest as chronic illness, arthritis, rheumatism and other forms of stiffness and congestion.
- A lack of self-confidence can hamper the ability to gain or keep a job. Often there is a reluctance to try new methods or to be sufficiently open-minded to keep up with new developments concerning work.
- A negative attitude may make them unpopular with co-workers and employers.
- Professional advancement may be hampered by rigidly organized structures or older, more established people who hold top positions. Older people may impose discipline and hard work on these people, which thwarts their freedom and self-confidence.
- Heavy burdens caused by the need to handle an estate or other matters related to inheritance. They may be saddled with the responsibility of caring for the elderly and sick.
- Difficulties and burdens concerning taxes, insurance, child support, spousal maintenance, or corporate money.

Saturn Inconjunct Uranus

These people may have difficulties in their job and health due to irregular and undisciplined habits concerning the daily work routine. They are capable of temporarily applying discipline to their work, but this is not sustained, and they are apt to move on for a new experience. Their enterprises and career endeavors may also suffer because of his lack of organization an a poor sense of timing.

They also have a tendency to be inconsistent in their attitudes. Often they expect discipline from others, while demanding freedom for themselves. They may be subjected to friends, employers, or coworkers who have the same tendencies.

In the case of well-organized people, this aspect may indicate that they will experience annoyance caused by people in their environment who are irregular, inconsiderate, and unpredictable in their conduct and performance of responsibilities.

In other cases, their duties and responsibilities do not allow for much personal freedom, and thus frustration affects the nervous system, causing ill health and tension.

Sudden accidents may cause bone breaks or other serious injuries.

Saturn Inconjunct Neptune

These people may possess a morose and pessimistic imagination that can interfere with healthy attitudes toward work and well-being. They are subject to psychosomatic complaints, and they may be plagued by chronic illnesses that are difficult to diagnose.

These chronic, psychological or physical illnesses may interfere with their ability to work. They can also suffer from fears of inadequacy or inferiority in meeting their responsibilities concerning work.

In some cases, the imagination creates problems where there are none. These morose tendencies are likely to alienate coworkers, employers, or other employees, or they may he hampered by association with people who have these problems.

There can also be a subtle, unconscious fear of death that prevents these people from leading a happy and productive life.

Peculiar difficulties and constraints may interfere with the acquisition of the things they need or feel they need in matters related to joint finances, insurance, taxes, or inheritance.

Saturn Inconjunct Pluto

These people can be hard and exacting taskmasters concerning work. They may be working diligently to improve the organization and efficiency of their work and surroundings, or they may be subjected to someone who makes heavy demands in these areas.

Their work may also involve a high degree of secrecy or considerable danger. It may even deal with matters of life and death. Their work may also relate to the areas of insurance, taxes, corporate finances, or estates and inheritance. (An funeral director is apt to have this aspect.)

There may be a preoccupation with death, causing a morose outlook on life, or they may be subjected to someone with such an attitude.

9

Natal Uranus

Inconjuncts involving Uranus in the natal chart can manifest in the following ways:

- Health difficulties that are caused by nervousness or erratic, unusual living and working habits.
- Difficulty in employment because of their unreliability and know-it-all attitude, or they may be subjected to someone with whom they works who has these tendencies.
- Sudden accidents and upsets may interfere with health and employment, resulting in difficulties relating to death, insurance, taxes and corporate money. In these matters, they may be misled by friends, or they may be the ones who mislead others.
- Friendships in the work environment can turn out to be a source of worry and irritation.

Uranus Inconjunct Neptune

This aspect indicates a generation of people who have difficult and stressful problems regarding their work, health, and management of joint resources. These people are apt to have a subtle fear and foreboding concerning their health and safety.

They also have an interest in death and life after death, and some will be drawn to psychology and investigate the forces of the unconscious and superconscious mind.

There is also an unconscious fear that if their motivations are not pure, they will experience failure. This comes from past evolutionary experiences.

The effect of this aspect will not be pronounced in the individual horoscope unless Uranus and Neptune are heavily aspected or angular.

Uranus Inconjunct Pluto

This aspect indicates a generation of people who have serious problems with issues involving life and death. This generation is also apt to be caught up in mass karmic events such as war or a natural catastrophe. Often they are forced to witness large-scale death and destruction.

The individual who has this aspect has energies that need to be channeled in creative, regenerative work. The job or career may prove to be a hazard to life.

There is a strong awareness of occult forces and the possible effects of their misuse. There is also a tendency to become involved with groups that deal with occult, secret, or revolutionary activities.

10

Natal Neptune

Inconjuncts involving Neptune in the natal chart can manifest in the following ways:

- Health difficulties caused by an indulgence in alcohol and/or drugs, and they are indicative of emotional and mental health. This often manifests as psychosomatic illnesses and hypochondria.
- Ill health may be used as a means to escape work and responsibility, and there can be unreliability and inefficiency concerning work. On the other hand, there may be people in the professional environment who have these undesirable traits.
- Improperly defined responsibilities and contracts may cause difficulties and fraud in insurance, taxes, child support, spousal maintenance, and corporate money. These people may perpetrate such fraud, or be the victims of it. Sometimes they are involved in both.

Neptune Inconjunct Pluto

This aspect indicates a generation of people who have strong, occult karma to work out regarding the understanding of death and regeneration.

This would necessitate working with powerful forces that have far-reaching karmic effects, while encouraging people to learn how to do this in a regenerative way.

11

Natal Pluto

Inconjuncts involving Pluto in the natal chart can manifest in the following ways:

- Health and work problems that are caused by the extremist attitudes and uncompromising, emotional stands of these people.
- Work may have occupational hazards that contain an element of danger and death. Often, work can involve atomic energy and its consequent dangers. Miners who are in danger of being killed by a cave-in are a good example of this.
- In some way, there will be acquainted with death and the affairs of the dead, because of the double eighth house connotation.
- The profession may involve secrecy, military matters, etc. In the work environment, there may be people who constantly tell these people how to improve their techniques or health. Or the reverse, where these people try to do the same to others.
- Difficulties experienced in health, work, insurance, taxes, legacies, and corporate money.

Part Two

The Transiting Inconjunct

12

The Transiting Inconjunct

As a transit, the 150° inconjunct aspect has an orb of one degree. The transit is also of the nature of Virgo, the sixth house, and Mercury, as well as Scorpio, the eighth house, Mars, Pluto, and Uranus.

This transit usually brings subtle difficulties during which the individuals feel somewhat helpless. In many cases, they must stand on the sidelines during situations of inefficiency and mismanagement that affect them adversely and over which they has no control.

Through these unpleasant experiences, they learn the value of efficiency and attention to detail, and possibly the responsibilities involved in handling ecological issues and waste products. As a result of these experiences, they gain insight into improved and more efficient ways of doing things.

Situations are likely to arise that affect their health, work, and manner of dress, in addition to those that cause old, familiar life situations to be destroyed prior to the creation of an entirely new set of circumstances. Through this, they learn the lesson of non-attachment and the ability to adjust to changing conditions.

When a transiting planet is in the house corresponding to the sign it rules in the natural zodiac, and if the sign that transiting planet rules is on the cusp of the house ruled by the same transiting planet in the natural zodiac, then the affairs of the two houses are connected in a manner similar to mutual reception.

13

Transits of the Sun

Transiting Sun Inconjunct Natal Sun

This indicates a period of difficulty and stress in self-expression, as well as the pursuit of social activities, pleasure, and romance. Difficulties could also arise concerning children, their education, or their health.

When considering the departing, Virgo-sixth house type of inconjunct, these people could be forced to deal with difficulties in creative self-expression. Problems could arise over matters of personal authority and in work situations. Health and work problems could interfere with social activities, romance, and creative self-expression. Personal authority may be undermined.

Social or work difficulties could arise over matters of clothing and personal appearance, such as inappropriate dress for a given situation. Frustrating minor difficulties could also arise in acquiring proper wearing apparel.

When considering the approaching, Scorpio-eighth house type of inconjunct, these people may be forced to relinquish old egotistical attitudes and personal opinions in order to consider the values of others. Difficulties could arise involving insurance, taxes, business investments, or inheritance over which the individual has no control.

Romantic and sexual problems could be experienced under this transit. Problems involving spousal maintenance or child support could cause difficulties at this time. Joint finances and financial affairs related to business partnerships could also be subject to difficulties and nuisance factors. Under this transit, it becomes obvious there is a need to regenerate one's attitudes toward self-expression, pursuit of pleasure, romance, sex, gambling, speculation, the handling of children, joint money, and other people's values.

Transiting Sun Inconjunct Natal Moon

This aspect indicates a period of difficulties and annoying problems in everyday affairs. These often relate to unexpected financial situations, or problems involving the opposite sex, and an incorrect attitude toward domestic problems and family affairs could bring unwanted difficulties. Attention to detail, emotional flexibility, and good organization in everyday affairs can lessen these problems.

When considering the departing, Virgo-sixth house type of inconjunct, the individual could be troubled by family health problems or by a lack of good organization and order in the home. Personal health could also be at a low ebb during this transit, and problems could arise because of incorrect diet or eating habits. A tendency to spend too much money on clothing could also be a source of difficulty. Financially, limitations could curtail social activities in the home or expenditures on food, clothing, and household items. Family difficulties or health problems could interfere with the individual's work. Emotional difficulties could arise in relationships with authority figures or through being thwarted in some manner in the pursuit of self-expression and pleasure.

When considering the approaching, Scorpio-eighth house type of inconjunct, the individual should develop an attitude of detachment where inevitable changes in business, domestic, and family affairs are concerned. Difficulties related to insurance, taxes, inheritance, spousal maintenance, child support, or business could arise at this time, interfering with the individual's domestic life and pursuit of pleasure. The individual may be forced to consider the attitudes of family members and others in the household. Emotional problems could arise in romantic and sexual relationships. Authority figures may express dissatisfaction with the individual and his or her attitude, or the individual could feel this way about authority figures. In any event, the individual may be forced to relinquish outworn emotional attitudes and habit patterns.

Transiting Moon inconjunct the natal Sun has the same significance as transiting Sun inconjunct the natal Moon; however, its effects are felt for only a few hours, as opposed to the two or more days of the Sun transit.

Transiting Sun Inconjunct Natal Mercury

This indicates a period of difficulty in matters related to work, health, and relationships with superiors. Disagreements over work methodologies could arise between the individual and those in authority, and a lack of attention to detail could have unpleasant consequences for the individual. Problems could arise in relationships with brothers, sisters, neighbors, and coworkers.

Inappropriate dress, personal appearance, speech, or communication could be a source of problems, or the individual could be annoyed by having to deal with those having such problems.

Health problems could be caused by incorrect diet. Difficulties could also arise concerning the education or health of children.

Unexpected problems could force a revision of plans and decisions. Care should be taken when trying to find locations, as the individual can be confused by lack of detailed information.

Problems could arise in matters related to transportation and communication. Interruptions or slowdowns in mail or shipments can cause difficulties in meeting work schedules. Work and pleasure can interfere with each other at this time and the individual will be forced to make a decision as to which is more important.

If Mercury is retrograde, these problems can be of more than just a passing annoyance; this is especially true if Mercury is stationary retrograde.

When considering the departing, Virgo-sixth house type of inconjunct, matters related to work, diet, health, communication, and transportation are of importance. Problems related to work methodology or responsibility are likely to be the main source of difficulty. These problems often involve health matters of some sort, or the problems could be related to clothing or lack of appropriate clothing when needed, thus causing embarrassment.

When considering the Scorpio-eighth house type of inconjunct, the individual may be forced to give up old decisions or ideas in the light of new circumstances. Transportation breakdowns could necessitate costly repairs, or even a new vehicle. There can be a temptation to use caustic language or sarcasm as a result of annoyance of one type or another. Problems could arise with business contracts or in matters related to joint finances. The individual could be faced with difficult decisions concerning business, insurance, taxes, joint money, or goods of the dead.

Problems or important changes could arise concerning children, their health, or education.

Important changes could force the individual to revise his or her thinking.

Transiting Mercury inconjunct the natal Sun has the same significance as transiting Sun inconjunct natal Mercury; however, it is usually of shorter duration, unless Mercury is retrograde or stationary, in which case the effects of this transit would have a greater influence.

Transiting Sun Inconjunct Natal Venus

This indicates a period of difficult adjustment in financial affairs, close personal relationships, marriage, and romance. Those involved in artistic endeavors could experience unexpected difficulties and complexities. Strict attention to detail must be maintained if success is to be assured. Work and health problems could interfere with pleasures and social life.

When considering the departing, Virgo-sixth house type of inconjunct, the individual should adhere to proper social dress and personal appearance so as to avoid awkward situations. Over-indulgence in food could lead to health problems. The individual could also suffer because of a lack of mental objectivity in close personal relationships, and emotional problems could also affect romantic relationships at this time. In addition, this could be a period of emotional problems involving children or their education. Poor judgment regarding emotional problems can interfere with work efficiency and practical responsibilities, and small factors affecting important relationships must be taken into account if harmony is to be maintained in the workplace and social arena. A realistic attitude is a must for all artistic, musical, or theatrical endeavors as details or unforeseen factors could interfere with success.

When considering the approaching, Scorpio-eighth house type of inconjunct, an attitude of detachment must be maintained to avoid emotional suffering in romantic or close personal relationships. Old conditions and situations involving romantic relationships, money, joint finances, children, and social status may be altered or taken away. If the individual is unable to see the potential for creative self-expression in the new situation, emotional suffering is often the result. During this transit, consideration for the needs and feelings of others will make it easier to maintain harmony in joint finances and business affairs. Sexual problems, health problems related to sex, and a lack of physical vitality could manifest at this time.

Transiting Venus inconjunct the natal Sun has the same significance as transiting Sun inconjunct natal Venus; however, it could last for a shorter or longer period of time, depending upon the speed of motion of Venus and whether Venus is direct, stationary, or retrograde in motion.

Transiting Sun Inconjunct Natal Mars

This indicates a period of annoyance and conflict with authority figures over work methodologies, diet, health, personal appearance, or business affairs.

There can be danger of accidents at work or while using tools or machinery, and this period is not conducive to harmony in romantic and social relationships. Frustrations and difficulties could arise through creative self-expression and through interaction with children. This is not a good time to speculate on the stock market or to engage in gambling.

When considering the departing, Virgo-sixth house type of inconjunct, anger and irritability are likely to arise from work-related problems. During this period it is especially important to think before rushing into action; doing otherwise could result in physical danger and loss of time and money. Lack of attention to detail could bring serious consequences. Safety precautions while on the job or while working with tools or equipment should be observed. The health of children should be carefully considered during this period. Problems could arise in connection with clothing.

When considering the approaching, Scorpio-eighth house type of inconjunct, ego conflicts over matters related to joint finances, business, taxes, insurance, inheritance, child support, or spousal maintenance could arise. Sexual problems, especially jealousy, could also arise under this transit. Unwise social and sexual activity could be a source of problems, especially if children are involved. This period calls for diplomacy without appeasement. Problems with authority figures could arise over the handling of corporate money. Business and financial pressures could interfere with the individual's pleasures and social life. Children could be willful and disobedient during this period. Problems and financial difficulties could come about through taxes and insurance.

Transiting Mars inconjunct natal Sun has the same significance as transiting Sun inconjunct natal Mars; however, it is of longer duration, especially if Mars is stationary or retrograde during the aspect.

Transiting Sun Inconjunct Natal Jupiter

This indicates a period of difficulty, often caused by over-expansion combined with a lack of attention to important details. The individual could assume an inflated sense of his own importance, which could cause problems with employers or others in the work environment. Work and social activities are likely to conflict with each other at this time.

This is not a favorable period for travel or seeking the assistance of educational, religious, or cultural institutions and their administrators. A tendency to overextend oneself through heavy personal commitments should be avoided at this time. Problems could also arise concerning children and their education, and there could be difficulties concerning religion and cultural beliefs and standards.

When considering the departing, Virgo-sixth house type of inconjunct, the individual may be hospitalized or may be confined to bed at home. The individual's conduct and appearance may be out of harmony with prevailing cultural standards or expectations. There could also be a tendency for extravagance in social activities or in dress. Expense of health-oriented regimes may prove to be less satisfactory than expected.

When considering the approaching type of Scorpio-eighth house inconjunct, the individual must exercise prudence and caution in business dealings or matters related to insurance, taxes, inheritance, financial matters related to divorce. Caution should also be exercised when dealing with religious or cultural institutions. This is a poor time to borrow money or to go into debt.

Transiting Jupiter inconjunct the natal Sun has the same effect as transiting Sun inconjunct natal Jupiter; however, it lasts for a longer period of time and indicates a sustained period of difficulty and adjustment.

Transiting Sun Inconjunct Natal Saturn

This indicates a period of difficulty caused by heavy responsibilities in career, business, and professional activities. Work responsibilities are apt to interfere with the care of children and social activities.

This is not a favorable time to seek employment or change jobs. Physical hardships, such as cold weather, could be a hindrance to work and self-expression. The individual should avoid a negative or pessimistic outlook during this transit. This is not a favorable period for romantic relationships or dealing with children, as heavy responsibilities or harsh attitudes can block the expression of warmth in relationships. Problems could arise with the employer, authority figures, or older people. Problems could also arise with old, unresolved conditions that could hinder self-expression.

When considering the departing, Virgo-sixth house type of inconjunct, the individual is likely to experience fatigue and lack of vitality. Inefficiency and administrative red tape can interfere with work progress.

When considering the approaching, Scorpio-eighth house type of inconjunct, problems and difficulties can arise related to business, taxes, insurance, inheritance, child support, spousal maintenance, and joint finances.

Transiting Saturn inconjunct the natal Sun has the same significance as the transiting Sun inconjunct natal Saturn; however, it lasts for a much longer period of time and indicates a sustained period of difficulties and heavy responsibilities.

Transiting Sun Inconjunct Natal Uranus

This indicates a time of unexpected difficulties in work, social, and romantic activities, and in dealings with children. There can also be difficulties with electronics and mechanical systems and devices, especially if they relate to the individual's work in some way.

Unexpected problems can also arise that affect the individual's friendships and group associations, as well as creative self-expression as it relates to these activities.

When considering the departing, Virgo-sixth house type of inconjunct, nervous disorders, unexpected problems and disruptions related to work, personal health, or the health of children can arise. This also applies to romantic relationships, friendships, and group associations.

When considering the approaching, Scorpio-eighth house type of inconjunct, the individual may have to deal with the unexpected death of friends or associates. Unexpected financial or corporate problems involving insurance, taxes, friends, groups, and organizations could also arise.

Transiting Uranus inconjunct the natal Sun has the same significance as the transiting Sun inconjunct natal Uranus; however, it lasts for a much longer period of time and indicates a sustained period of need to adjust to unexpected difficulties and problems.

Transiting Sun Inconjunct Natal Neptune

This indicates a period of difficult to diagnose illnesses and difficult to define problems at work. Confusion and deception could arise around romantic and social activities as well as matters related to children. This is not a favorable time to be hospitalized or institutionalized. Sources of confusion beyond the individual's control interfere with his or her self-expression.

When considering the departing, Virgo-sixth house type of inconjunct, the individual could be subject to strange viral illnesses or subtle environmental hazards dangerous to the health. Confusing factors can influence the individual's work and make it difficult to efficiently handle job tasks. He or she may have to deal with people who are psychologically disturbed or ill.

This is not a favorable time for travel or for mystical or occult practices. The individual could be subject to confinement because of ill health, and frustration in creative self-expression could result in a psychosomatic illness.

When considering the approaching, Scorpio-eighth house type of inconjunct, the individual should avoid risky financial ventures and guard against hidden flaws in financial investments, business activities, and matters related to insurance, taxes, and joint finances. In some cases, there could be the mysterious death of someone of consequence to the individual, especially if this transit is reinforced by other indications.

Transiting Neptune inconjunct the natal Sun has the same significance as the transiting Sun inconjunct natal Neptune; however, it is of longer duration and indicates a sustained period of confusion and self-deception.

Transiting Sun Inconjunct Natal Pluto

This indicates a period of potentially drastic changes in personal circumstances, especially those related to work, health, children, and social, romantic, and business activities.

Occupational hazards can be a serious threat to the individual's health and safety. The necessity for drastic revisions could influence matters related to children, romance, social activities, and creative self-expression.

When considering the departing, Virgo-sixth house type of inconjunct, the individual could be threatened by serious health problems. He or she may also be subject to involuntary work of some form or another.

When considering the approaching, Scorpio-eighth house type of inconjunct, ecological or environmental issues could affect the individual in a personal way and threaten health and security. Situations of war, and other situations of danger, could affect the personal life. These threats are all the more serious if the individual has an adverse natal Pluto-Sun aspect. Difficulties are likely to arise over joint finances, inheritance, taxes, child support, or spousal maintenance.

Transiting Pluto inconjunct the natal Sun has the same significance as the transiting Sun inconjunct natal Pluto; however, its effects are longer lasting and more severe.

14

Transits of the Moon

Transiting Moon Inconjunct Natal Sun

See Transiting Sun Inconjunct Natal Moon.

Transiting Moon Inconjunct Natal Moon

This indicates a period of petty annoyances in domestic and family affairs. Problems could arise with household finances and domestic chores, and the individual or a family member could experience an emotional upset. This is not a favorable time for dealing with women or involvement in sensitive emotional issues. Care should be exercised in diet in order to avoid indigestion or other minor physical problems.

When considering the departing, Virgo-sixth house type of inconjunct, the individual could experience a brief conflict between work and domestic responsibilities.

When considering the approaching, Scorpio-eighth house type of inconjunct, emotional frustrations and financial difficulty could cause temporary problems.

Transiting Moon Inconjunct Natal Mercury

This indicates a period of concern with everyday chores and matters affecting diet and health. Delayed or confused communication can be a source of irritation, and lack of attention to detail can cause inefficiency and frustration in everyday tasks. The individual could be frustrated in communication with women or the public in general.

Inappropriate dress and lack of attention to proper hygiene (including household cleanliness) could have undesirable consequences for the individual.

When considering the departing, Virgo-sixth house type of inconjunct, the planet Mercury is strongly emphasized because of its rulership of Virgo and the natural sixth house. Therefore, a logical, systematic approach to everyday tasks in the home and at work is needed; otherwise, confusion, inefficiency, and frustration will be the result. This aspect is often associated with health, diet, and work difficulties.

When considering the approaching, Scorpio-eighth house type of inconjunct, the individual may have to accept change in everyday affairs. It may be necessary to detoxify or to eliminate a toxic condition in the body that interferes with normal health or work. A greater degree of detachment may be required in emotional relationships with women or family members. Unexpected financial difficulties could arise as a result of ill health or other factors that interfere with work. Caution should be exercised in signing contracts or making business agreements.

Transiting Mercury inconjunct the natal Moon has the same significance as the transiting Moon inconjunct natal Mercury; however, it lasts for a longer period of time, the length of which depends upon the speed of Mercury and whether it is direct, retrograde or stationary. If Mercury is stationary while making this transit, the problems with which the individual must deal may have long-term significance.

Transiting Moon Inconjunct Natal Venus

This indicates problems and frustrations in everyday family and in romantic and emotional relationships. Confusion and difficulties in the domestic arena and with social activities can bring upsets, misunderstandings, and hurt feelings. Financial problems affecting family affairs and social activities can create helpless and frustrating conditions that interfere with the individual's happiness and emotional well-being. During this period, the individual should bear in mind that happiness should not be dependent on material prosperity. Excessive indulgence in sweet or rich food should be avoided during this transit.

When considering the departing, Virgo-sixth house type of inconjunct, emotional and financial problems should be handled through a precise, impartial, analytical assessment of the situation, combined with communication. Practical service in helping others may be necessary in order to ease mental stress and emotional tension. The individual's work and personal relationships could be subject to worry and financial problems.

When considering the approaching, Scorpio-eighth house type of inconjunct, emotional detachment is necessary for harmony in family affairs and close relationships. Under this transit, the individual can learn that he or she can always freely express and receive love, and that it cannot demanded it of others. Caution should be exercised in financial affairs, especially if they involve joint money, insurance, taxes, divorce-related finances, or inheritance. Unnecessary expenditures should be avoided during this transit. There could be a severance of old emotional attachments. This can often be a traumatic experience unless the individual has learned that personal freedom can only be exercised if others are allowed the same freedom. In any event, situations of jealousy and attempts to make others feel guilty should be avoided.

Transiting Venus inconjunct the natal Moon has the same significance as the transiting Moon inconjunct natal Venus; however, it lasts for a longer period of time, which varies depending on the speed of Venus and whether it is direct, retrograde, or stationary.

Transiting Moon Inconjunct Natal Mars

This indicates a period of emotional irritation resulting from petty annoyances and disturbances in everyday affairs. This often annoys the individual or those around him or her to the point of anger. Emotional upsets can interfere with the digestion, bringing pain and discomfort; the cliche, "being sick to one's stomach," about a situation is typical of this transit. Emotional irritations of this type can also arise because of financial problems and worries.

Precautions should be taken to avoid the danger of domestic accidents and fire at this time.

When considering the departing, Virgo-sixth house type of inconjunct, illness caused by inflammation and infections can occur. Occupational hazards that could cause illness or injury should be carefully avoided, as should emotional confrontations with employers or coworkers. Damage to clothing or other personal effects could become a problem, and conflicts could arise over family finances and domestic and work responsibilities.

When considering the approaching Scorpio-eighth house type of inconjunct, difficulties related to insurance, taxes, corporate money, child support, spousal maintenance, inheritance, and family finances could be a major source of irritation. Any attempt to emotionally dominate or coerce others should be avoided, and this is not a favorable period to handle important business affairs. The individual could have difficulties in dealing with the opposite sex at this time. This transit sometimes coincides with the death of a family member or of someone important to the individual. Extra precautions should be taken to avoid potentially dangerous situations at this time.

Transiting Mars inconjunct the natal Moon has the same significance as the transiting Moon inconjunct natal Mars; however, it lasts for a longer period of time, which varies according to the speed of Mars' motion and whether Mars is direct, retrograde, or stationary. During this period the individual must be willing to relinquish outworn resentments and emotional attitudes.

Transiting Moon Inconjunct Natal Jupiter

This indicates a period of emotional confusion and misplaced sympathy. Rich foods and incorrect dietary habits can cause indigestion or other health problems during this transit, and there is a tendency to commit to more responsibilities than can be adequately handled. Lack of attention to detail can have an undermining effect on the individual in his or her career and personal lives. There may even be a tendency for hypochondria at this time.

Unnecessary financial expenditures that could lead to later difficulties should be avoided under this transit.

Family problems could arise over differences in moral, educational, and cultural philosophies.

Difficulties could arise while traveling or residing in a faraway place, and financial affairs related to long-distance commerce could be less than satisfactory at this time.

When considering the departing Virgo-sixth house type of inconjunct, the individual should avoid indifference to personal and household hygiene, as well as diet. Emotional problems over religious, education, and cultural standards could arise in the individual's work situation. Efficiency and thrift in domestic, financial, and work affairs is necessary to relieve any stress in these areas at this time.

When considering the approaching Scorpio-eighth house type of inconjunct, the individual should avoid using deceptive tactics, as well as being aware of potential deception in religious, business, and corporate financial dealings. Conflict could arise over inheritance, divorce-related financial matters, and family finances, and emotionalism and sentimentality could distort the individual's judgment in these matters.

Transiting Jupiter inconjunct the natal Moon has the same significance as the transiting Moon inconjunct natal Jupiter; however, it lasts for a longer period of time, which varies according to the speed of Jupiter's motion and whether Jupiter is direct, retrograde, or stationary.

Transiting Moon Inconjunct Natal Saturn

This period is usually one associated with a disgruntled and dissatisfied attitude. Adequate rest and proper diet are very important.

When considering the departing Virgo-sixth house type of inconjunct, health and work problems are likely to be the major issues. The individual may be required to take responsibility for the care of an elderly or disabled family member, or need to assume some of the business or professional responsibilities of family members. Wearing apparel, the lack of proper clothes or money problems related of clothing could also be a problem.

When considering the approaching Scorpio-eighth house type of inconjunct, the individual may be forced to relinquish old emotional attitudes and attachments, especially in regard to home and family affairs. Hardships in these areas may force the individual to reevaluate his or her sense of values. The financial difficulties of family members, as well as friends, could also be a problem.

Transiting Saturn inconjunct the natal Moon has the same significance as the transiting Moon inconjunct natal Saturn; however, it lasts for a longer period of time and, therefore, is more serious in its effects.

Transiting Moon Conjunct Natal Uranus

This indicates a period of disruptive change in financial, family, and domestic affairs. The individual could experience sudden difficulties and situations in which he or she feels helpless; these situations could relate to financial affairs, taxes, death, insurance, or corporate affairs. Sudden, peculiar, and disturbing psychic experiences could occur at this time. Emotional problems could arise over sex, family relationships, friends, and group and organizational affairs. The individual's family could disapprove of his or her friends and group associates. Family, friends, groups, and organizations could make sudden and unusual financial demands on the individual. This is an unfavorable time to experiment with diets and food fads as emotional confusion and nervousness could interfere with digestion during this transit.

When considering the departing Virgo-sixth house type of inconjunct, sudden changes in the work environment and health are apt to become a problem.

When considering the approaching Scorpio-eighth house type of inconjunct, business and financial problems or the unexpected death of a family member or friend could cause problems. However, this is more likely to be the case when transiting Uranus is inconjunct the natal Moon.

Transiting Uranus inconjunct the natal Moon has the same significance as the transiting Moon inconjunct natal Uranus; however, it lasts for a longer period of time, indicating a sustained period of emotional, family and financial upsets and confusion.

Transiting Moon Inconjunct Natal Neptune

This indicates a period of psychological confusion caused by subconscious forces the individual usually does not recognize or understand. Health problems due to incorrect dietary habits, drugs, or alcohol can arise, and the individual may have to deal with emotionally-disturbed family members. Deception or confusion over financial affairs can deplete the individual at this time.

Emotional confusion is likely to interfere with the individual's work efficiency, and there is a tendency to experience disturbing psychic influences during this period. The individual could be subject to psychosomatic or difficult-to-diagnose illnesses during this period. This is an unfavorable period for dealing with hospitals and institutions, and caution should be exercised in the use of drugs and anaesthesia. This is not a favorable time to dabble in psychic or occult practices, because of the danger of deception and undesirable astral influences.

When considering the departing Virgo-sixth house type of inconjunct, family mental health problems, peculiar illnesses, and emotional difficulties that interfere with work efficiency are apt to deplete the vitality and affect the health of the individual.

When considering the approaching Scorpio-eighth house type of inconjunct, deception in financial affairs and undesirable psychic influences are likely to be the major source of difficulty. The individual should guard against deception in business and financial dealings.

Transiting Neptune inconjunct the natal Moon has the same significance as the transiting Moon inconjunct natal Neptune; however, it lasts for a much longer period of time.

Transiting Moon Inconjunct Natal Pluto

This indicates a period during which the individual feels inadequate and helpless to deal with ongoing emotional and financial disruption. Secrecy or coercion in financial affairs should be avoided during this transit.

Circumstances over which the individual has no control could force relocation or a change in family relationships or business dealings. Difficult circumstances are likely to arise involving taxes, insurance, corporate money, child support, spousal maintenance, and joint finances.

The individual may be forced to give up old habit patterns and attitudes regarding family relationships, money, and domestic affairs, and this is a difficult period for dealing with women.

When considering the departing Virgo-sixth house type of inconjunct, health problems, occupational hazards, and ecological concerns are of special importance.

When considering the approaching Scorpio-eighth house type of inconjunct, death, business and financial affairs, and undesirable psychic influences are likely to be a major source of difficulty.

Transiting Pluto inconjunct the natal Moon has the same significance as the transiting Moon inconjunct natal Pluto; however, because it lasts off and on for a year or longer, as opposed to the few hours of the Moon transit, it is of far greater importance and brings about major and irrevocable changes in the individual's outlook. It is important to avoid large crowds or mobs during this transit, as one can become a casualty in such situations. When transiting Pluto is inconjunct the natal Moon, the death of a family member or someone of emotional importance can adversely affect the individual.

15

Transits of Mercury

Transiting Mercury Inconjunct Natal Sun

See Transiting Sun Inconjunct Natal Mercury.

Transiting Mercury Inconjunct Natal Moon

See Transiting Moon Inconjunct Natal Mercury.

Transiting Mercury Inconjunct Natal Mercury

This indicates a period of nervousness and detailed problems related to health and work. Communication breakdowns, transportation problems, and delays in mail and shipments are also likely to interfere with work and efficiency. The individual could also be confronted with difficulties related to clothing and hygiene, or inappropriate dress could be a problem. Orderliness and cleanliness in the working and living environment may need attention. Problems could arise in communication with brothers, sisters, neighbors, and coworkers.

When considering the departing Virgo-sixth house type of inconjunct, health and work problems will be of major concern

When considering the approaching Scorpio-eighth house type of inconjunct, the individual is likely to be faced with difficult problems related to business, corporate money, and the handling of collective resources. Brothers, sisters, neighbors, friends, and coworkers could be involved in these problems. Ecological concerns and issues could also involve the individual at this time.

Transiting Mercury Inconjunct Natal Venus

This indicates a period of communication difficulties involving business, money, partnerships, marriage, and social and romantic relationships. Issues concerning dress and social situations could arise, as could matters related to art, music, entertainment, advertising, social activities, and public relations. Emotional problems could arise involving communications with brothers, sisters, friends, neighbors, coworkers, marriage, and business partners. These emotional upsets are likely to interfere with the individual's work efficiency. There is also the tendency to engage in idle social chatter while on the job, which interferes with more important duties.

When considering the departing Virgo-sixth house type of inconjunct, incorrect eating habits, and emotional upsets that interfere with work are likely to be a source of difficulty during this period.

When considering the approaching Scorpio-eighth house type of inconjunct, problems related to financial and sexual matters are likely to be the source of difficulty.

Transiting Venus inconjunct natal Mercury has the same significance as transiting Mercury inconjunct natal Venus; however, it usually lasts for a slightly longer period of time, depending on whether Venus or Mercury is stationary or retrograde or fast in motion.

Transiting Mercury Inconjunct Natal Mars

This indicates a period of potential difficulty with infections, environmental irritations, petty annoyances, and occupational hazards. The individual is likely to be short-tempered and irritable at this time. Particular caution should be exercised in the use of knives, sharp instruments, machinery, and guns as impatience and irritation can increase the danger of accidents, especially while driving. This is an unfavorable time to sign contracts and to make agreements or important decisions. The individual should guard against caustic and sarcastic speech, which could cause disharmony in the working environment and eventually upset the health. Environmental pollution and occupational hazards could cause health problems.

When considering the departing Virgo-sixth house type of inconjunct, communication problems and disagreements over work-related matters are likely to arise. Health problems caused by nervousness, irritation, and lack of safety precautions could result in problems. This is a poor time to change jobs, seek employment, and purchase clothes. Medical problems, possibly involving the decision to undergo surgery, could develop at this time.

When considering the approaching Scorpio-eighth house type of inconjunct, difficult decisions related to financial affairs, insurance, taxes, inheritance, joint finances and collective resources could arise.

Transiting Mars inconjunct natal Mercury has the same significance as transiting Mercury inconjunct natal Mars; however, it lasts for a longer period of time and indicates a sustained period of nervousness, irritability, and work-related problems.

Transiting Mercury Inconjunct Natal Jupiter

This indicates a period of confusion and indecision regarding matters related to work, health, education, religion, travel, and dealings with those from or in faraway places. There is a tendency for the individual to underestimate the amount of time, energy, money, and work required to realize what he or she envisions. There is a tendency to ignore or overlook practical details, which could result in problems and inefficiencies, especially in work. Transportation and communication involving distant places, educational and religious ideas, institutions, foreigners or foreign countries, siblings, neighbors, friends or coworkers could be a source of difficulty at this time.

When considering the departing Virgo-sixth house type of inconjunct, problems related to work and health are likely to be of concern; education, travel and religion are likely to be involved in some way. Legal red tape and institutional formality may interfere with efficiency.

When considering the approaching Scorpio-eighth house type of inconjunct, difficulties related to legal affairs, travel, higher education, and dealing with institutions can affect the individual's business and joint finances.

Transiting Jupiter inconjunct natal Mercury has the same significance as transiting Mercury inconjunct natal Jupiter; however, it lasts for a longer period of time, depending on the motion of Jupiter and whether it is direct, stationary, or retrograde. This transit occurs twice in the twelve-year-cycle of Jupiter and indicates a period when practicality and reality are needed in work, health, education, and religious and cultural activities.

Transiting Mercury Inconjunct Natal Saturn

This indicates a period of pessimism, worry, nervous strain, and problems in work. During this period the individual often has to work twice as hard to achieve results. A negative or pessimistic outlook can interfere with finding solutions to problems in work and health, and communication problems are likely to arise with older and more established people, superiors, government agencies or those in positions of power and authority. This is a poor time to present new ideas for consideration. The individual is often forced to revise and reevaluate old decisions in business and work.

Rigid governmental or institutional procedures and red tape can interfere with efficiency and creativity in work, and the individual should employ a flexible and optimistic mental outlook in dealing with problems at this time. This is a poor time to seek employment, change jobs, or formulate business contracts and agreements. It is best to maintain the status quo, take care of routine responsibilities and wait for a more favorable period to make changes.

When considering the departing Virgo-sixth house type of

inconjunct, susceptibility to illness, worry, and an oppressive work load are likely to be major sources of difficulty. The individual could be plagued with difficult-to-fulfill contracts and agreements. Care should be exercised to protect the health during this period as there are likely to be irritations due to skin, bone, or dental problems. Worry, anxiety, and overwork can have an undermining effect on the individual's health.

When considering the approaching Scorpio-eighth house type of inconjunct, problems related to business, joint finances, taxes, insurance, and corporate affairs are likely to cause problems. The individual may be forced to relinquish old mental attitudes and preconceptions. There may be a need to find new and more efficient ways to handle business communication.

Transiting Saturn inconjunct natal Mercury has the same significance as transiting Mercury inconjunct natal Saturn; however, it lasts for a much longer period of time and indicates a sustained period of heavy work and difficult problems and responsibilities. This transit occurs twice in the twenty-nine-year-cycle of Saturn.

Transiting Mercury Inconjunct Natal Uranus

This indicates a time of sudden and unexpected disruptions in routine work matters, business communication, and normal daily procedures. The individual, or those with whom he or she must deal, may display erratic and unpredictable behavior that interferes with the normal flow of work and communication. This is not a favorable time to formulate contracts or agreements or to make plans, as unexpected factors are likely to arise which interfere with the original planning and idea.

Technical difficulties, especially involving electronics, mobile devices, and computers, can disrupt the normal flow of business and work. Nervousness and mental irritations can cause difficulty in what are normally harmonious interchanges with siblings, neighbors, friends, coworkers, and group associates. This is not a favorable time to initiate new and untried methods of doing things.

When considering the departing Virgo-sixth house type of

inconjunct, the individual is likely to experience sudden, unexpected problems in work, health, transportation, and communication. These problems could involve equipment malfunctions, especially electronic equipment.

When considering the approaching Scorpio-eighth house type of inconjunct, sudden problems are likely to arise involving business and financial communications and decision-making. There could also be a tendency to entertain impractical notions involving science and the occult. Friends, groups and organizations could present problems to the individual at this time.

Transiting Uranus inconjunct natal Mercury has the same significance as transiting Mercury in conjunct natal Uranus; however, it is of much longer duration and presents serious problems of more than passing significance. This transit occurs twice in the average life span.

Transiting Mercury Inconjunct Natal Neptune

This indicates a period of mental confusion, deception, and muddle that affects business, work, health, transportation, and communication with siblings, neighbors, friends, work, group and business associates. This is a poor time to sign contracts, formulate agreements or make decisions, as hidden factors could cause plans to go awry. The individual's mental clarity and judgment could be distorted by unconscious forces of which he or she is not aware, and judgment could be impaired because of incorrect, distorted, or incomplete information. Psychological problems could interfere with work efficiency at this time.

The individual could be subject to psychosomatic or difficult-to-diagnose illnesses. Drugs and alcohol or other escapist tendencies are especially likely to interfere with clarity of judgment and work efficiency. Discipline is needed to keep one's attention to the job at hand, especially when driving.

Confused communication and procrastination in handling work and correspondence could undermine the individual's business and work.

When considering the departing Virgo-sixth house type of inconjunct, psychosomatic illnesses, psychological problems, and confused communication can interfere with the individual's work and health.

When considering the approaching Scorpio-eighth house type of inconjunct, lack of clarity in thought and handling communication can cause problems in business and finances. The individual could entertain peculiar and impractical religious ideas or be subject to undesirable astral influences.

Transiting Neptune inconjunct natal Mercury has the same significance as transiting Mercury inconjunct natal Neptune; however, it lasts for a much longer period of time. Consequently, it is more serious in its effect. This transit occurs only once or twice in an average life span.

Transiting Mercury Inconjunct Natal Pluto

This indicates a period of serious problems involving work, business, and health that demand important decisions of far-reaching consequence. The individual is often forced to revise his or her work methodologies, transportation, and communications. Health problems could arise that in extreme cases could threaten the individual's life; these often result from occupational hazards and environmental pollution. Extreme caution is recommended in any use of advanced technologies. The individual should avoid mental coercion of others, as well as allowing others to do the same.

This transit can improve insight, mental power, and discipline; however, the individual usually undergoes serious mental strain and tension. Problems could arise and decisions would have to be made regarding insurance, taxes, corporate money, divorce-related finances, and joint finances. This is not a favorable time for unwise occult or psychic experimentations.

The individual could become mentally preoccupied with sex or matters related to sex, causing nervousness and an ill-at-ease feeling.

When considering the departing Virgo-sixth house type of

inconjunct, serious decisions and difficult problems are likely to arise concerning work and health.

When considering the approaching, Scorpio-eighth house type of inconjunct, reevaluation of serious business and financial matters come to the fore.

Transiting Pluto inconjunct natal Mercury has the same significance as transiting Mercury inconjunct natal Pluto; however, it lasts off and on for a year or longer and is of far greater importance and consequence. This transit occurs only once or twice in the average life span.

16

Transits of Venus

Transiting Venus Inconjunct Natal Sun
See Transiting Sun Inconjunct Natal Venus.

Transiting Venus Inconjunct Natal Moon
See Transiting Moon Inconjunct Natal Venus.

Transiting Venus Inconjunct Natal Mercury
See Transiting Mercury Inconjunct Natal Venus.

Transiting Venus Inconjunct Natal Venus
This indicates a period of frustration in financial, romantic, social, and marital affairs. Difficulties could arise because of conflicts between work responsibilities and romantic or social activities. Excessive socializing on the job could interfere with work efficiency. Wrong dietary habits could impair the individual's health. Sexual overindulgence could also have an adverse effect on the individual's health and well-being.

Difficult and frustrating circumstances could interfere with romantic or social fulfillment. Emotional frustrations are apt to make the individual feel dissatisfied and unhappy.

When considering the departing Virgo-sixth house type of inconjunct, the individual is likely to experience conflict between work responsibilities and social or pleasurable pursuits. Socializing in the work environment could cause problems; however, social or romantic opportunities could come through the workplace.

When considering the approaching Scorpio-eighth house type of inconjunct, sexual and financial problems are likely to be the major source of concern.

Transiting Venus Inconjunct Natal Mars

This indicates the possibility of health problems related to sex, romance, and business and financial affairs. Romantic frustration can lead to anger and unhappiness, and jealousy can be a problem. This is a poor time to change jobs and for financial dealings.

This is not a good period for business or financial dealings involving art, entertainment, or luxury items. Circumstances could arise where the feelings of the individual, or those with whom he or she is connected, could be hurt in some way. Consideration and diplomacy are needed in all close relationships, and especially in situations that involve work or practical responsibilities.

When considering the departing Virgo-sixth house type of inconjunct, the individual should avoid emotional confrontations in work situations, and exercise good judgment in health matters.

When considering the approaching Scorpio-eighth house type of inconjunct, sexual problems and matters related to money and business are likely to be the major source of difficulty, especially in romantic, business, or marital partnerships.

Transiting Mars inconjunct natal Venus has the same significance as transiting Venus inconjunct natal Mars; however, it usually lasts for a longer period of time and can indicate serious emotional problems.

Transiting Venus Inconjunct Natal Jupiter

This indicates a period of annoyance with inconsequential social niceties and insincere gestures of kindness or friendliness.

Self-indulgent tendencies can become a problem at this time. Hence, this is not the best time to deal with social, educational, religious, or cultural institutions. The individual may seek to avoid work responsibilities through involvement in inconsequential social actions, and a tendency for financial extravagance should be curbed at this time.

A false sense of security and optimism can result in laxity where important details are concerned.

When considering the departing Virgo-sixth house type of inconjunct, escapist tendencies where practical responsibilities are concerned could create problems. Excessive eating or overindulgence in the wrong foods can adversely affect the health.

When considering the approaching Scorpio-eighth house type of inconjunct, unnecessary extravagance in business dealings should be avoided. The individual could be wasteful or extravagant in the use of money and other resources.

Transiting Jupiter inconjunct natal Venus has the same significance as transiting Venus inconjunct natal Jupiter; however, it lasts for a longer period of time and indicates the possibility of more serious self-indulgence and extravagance. This transit occurs twice in the twelve-year-cycle of Jupiter.

Transiting Venus Inconjunct Natal Saturn

This indicates a period of romantic, social, and emotional loneliness and frustration, when heavy work responsibilities could interfere with social and romantic fulfillment. The individual could develop a hard, unsympathetic attitude toward others, or be subjected to such treatment, and responsibility for caring for an older person could interfere with social and professional activity.

The individual could be subject to irksome financial difficulties in business. Lack of money is also likely to interfere with pleasures, luxuries, and social activities.

When considering the departing Virgo-sixth house type of inconjunct, conflict between personal pleasures and work responsibilities are likely to be the main concern.

When considering the approaching Scorpio-eighth house type of inconjunct, the individual can experience limitations in business and financial affairs. There could also be the termination of an old social or romantic relationship, a severance that could make the individual feel lonely and unhappy.

Transiting Saturn inconjunct natal Venus has the same significance as transiting Venus inconjunct natal Saturn; however, it lasts for a longer period of time and indicates a sustained period of financial limitation and romantic and emotional frustration. This occurs twice in the twenty-nine-year cycle of Saturn.

Transiting Venus Inconjunct Natal Uranus

This indicates a period in which the individual experiences instability in romantic and marital relationships. Partnerships and friendships are apt to be stressful due to money and work-related issues, and romantic and sexual relationships are strained. Sexual experimentation could result in serious health problems.

Financial problems can arise that involve friendships, groups, corporate money, joint finances, insurance, inheritance, taxes, child support, and spousal maintenance.

When considering the departing Virgo-sixth house type of inconjunct, the individual should avoid unnecessary social activity that could be detrimental to health or work. There could be a tendency toward meaningless social activity with friends and others. Work responsibilities and romantic and social activities could interfere with each other. Ostentatiousness or eccentric dress could provoke criticism and disapproval at this time.

When considering the approaching, Scorpio-eighth house type of inconjunct, the individual should avoid unnecessary expenditures and involvement in unstable business or financial endeavors; this is especially true in matters related to taxes, insurance, inheritance, and joint money. At this time, the individual could be prone to intense sexual involvements that could somehow affect personal resources. Unnecessary expenditures on luxuries and romantic and social activities could cause problems.

Transiting Uranus inconjunct natal Venus has the same significance as transiting Venus inconjunct natal Uranus; however, it lasts off and on for a year or longer, indicating a sustained period of unstable romantic, social, sexual, and financial problems.

Transiting Venus Inconjunct Natal Neptune

This indicates a period of emotional confusion in social, romantic, and financial affairs. The individual is likely to be emotionally sensitive, and so much so as to overreact to imagined or unintended slights in close personal relationships. Unsuitable and unstable romantic involvements are possible. Beware of the danger of deception in social and business dealings. The individual could adopt a hedonistic tendency in order to avoid unpleasant situations and responsibilities, which could take the form of psychological daydreaming or wool-gathering. Artists and musicians could receive intuitive inspiration at this time, although they could have difficulty in bringing this inspiration into concrete manifestation.

In general, one should guard against self-deception and unrealistic attitudes in close relationships and financial dealings. Misplaced sympathies can also lead to difficulties under this transit.

When considering the departing Virgo-sixth house type of inconjunct, emotional problems, tendencies to inertia and confusion in social, romantic, and financial matters are likely to interfere with the individual's health and efficiency in work.

When considering the approaching Scorpio-eighth house type of inconjunct, the individual may have to learn a lesson of detachment with respect to romantic or other important relationships.

Transiting Neptune inconjunct natal Venus has the same significance as transiting Venus inconjunct natal Neptune; however, it generally lasts off and on for a year or so, indicating a sustained period of difficult emotional adjustments.

Transiting Venus Inconjunct Natal Pluto

This indicates a period during which important, and sometimes irrevocable, changes can occur in romantic, social, business, and financial affairs, and could involve the severance of old relationships and establishing new ones. In these matters, the individual should avoid the use of coercive tactics and not allow to do the same. Sexual problems could arise that would be difficult to resolve. Sensitivity and consideration in close personal relationships is a must if harmony is to be maintained.

This can be a good period for self-improvement in artistic or musical expression. The individual may take an interest in improving the work environment. During this period the individual may be forced to reexamine his or her desires and emotional tendencies, and could become involved in corporate business dealing with art, music, entertainment, or luxury items. The individual is also vulnerable to social diseases during this period, especially if other indications concur.

When considering the departing Virgo-sixth house type of inconjunct, sexual or personal relationship problems can interfere with work and health.

When considering the approaching Scorpio-eighth house type of inconjunct, an attitude of detachment to emotional issues affecting close personal relationships is necessary. Justice and fairness is essential to the successful handling of business dealings during this transit.

Transiting Pluto inconjunct natal Venus has the same significance as transiting Venus inconjunct natal Pluto; however, it lasts off and on for a year or longer, indicating a sustained period of important and irrevocable changes in the social, romantic and financial affairs of the individual's life.

17

Transits of Mars

Transiting Mars Inconjunct Natal Sun

See Transiting Sun Inconjunct Natal Mars.

Transiting Mars Inconjunct Natal Moon

See Transiting Moon Inconjunct Natal Mars.

Transiting Mars Inconjunct Natal Mercury

See Transiting Mercury Inconjunct Natal Mars.

Transiting Mars Inconjunct Natal Venus

See Transiting Venus Inconjunct Natal Mars.

Transiting Mars Inconjunct Natal Mars

This indicates a frustrating period where personal desires and actions are concerned. The individual is apt to become irritable and angry because of being confronted by difficult circumstances that are not under his or her direct personal control. Impulsive, ill-considered actions can have undesirable effects in work, business, and professional affairs. Carelessness in the working environment can result in accidents and injuries. Patience must be exercised if the above dangers are to be avoided.

When considering the departing Virgo-sixth house type of inconjunct, the individual must exercise caution and good judgment in matters affecting work and health.

When considering the approaching Scorpio-eighth house type of inconjunct, problems and conflicts can arise over joint finances, insurance, taxes, child support, and spousal maintenance.

Transiting Mars Inconjunct Natal Jupiter

This indicates a period of difficulties resulting from over-commitment and taking on responsibilities that are beyond the scope of available time and resources. There is also a tendency for ill-considered actions and wasted resources.

At this time the individual could aggressively promote his or her personal religious, cultural, educational, or political beliefs, thereby annoying and alienating others, or he could be subjected to such treatment. Biased moral judgments that favor personal desires are likely to cause problems, especially where work and business affairs are concerned.

During this period, the individual is often forced into an awareness of detailed responsibilities that have been glossed over and now must be meticulously handled before further progress can be made. Disagreements over religious, cultural, or moral standards are likely to cause problems in business, financial affairs, and the work area. Breakdowns in domestic appliances or family affairs could tax the individual.

When considering the departing, Virgo-sixth house type of inconjunct, the individual is likely to run into problems with health or work caused by attempts to handle too much at once.

When considering the approaching Scorpio-eighth house type of inconjunct, the individual must be willing to relinquish personal desires, opinions, and expectations if the circumstances indicate such demands.

Transiting Jupiter inconjunct natal Mars has the same significance as transiting Mars inconjunct natal Jupiter; however, it generally lasts for a longer period of time, indicating a longer period during which the individual must analyze and correct his or her desires and actions with respect to the needs and realities of the larger social context.

Transiting Mars Inconjunct Natal Saturn

This indicates a period of hard work, stress, and difficulty in the individual's work and professional affairs. Harsh, practical realities tend to interfere with the individual's desires and action, often resulting in frustration and anger, which can engender a harsh, unsympathetic attitude toward others. On the other hand, the individual could be subjected to such treatments. Accidents and health hazards can occur in the work area during this period, so special caution is required in the use or handling of sharp instruments, machinery, and fire. Health problems arising at this time are apt to relate to the muscles, skin, ears, bones, and teeth, and vulnerable areas could be the head, knees, ankles, muscles, and sexual organs. In situations of war or potential violence, the individual should be extremely careful to avoid injury and possible death.

This is a poor time for important dealings with older, established people, authority figures, and the boss.

Chronic problems and difficulties in the individual's life could be aggravated at this time.

When considering the departing Virgo-sixth house type of inconjunct, the individual is likely to encounter heavy work loads, problems at work, and health difficulties.

When considering the approaching Scorpio-eighth house type of inconjunct, the individual could be drawn into power struggles and problems related to business, professional, and financial affairs. These problems could include insurance, inheritance, and corporate money.

Transiting Saturn inconjunct natal Mars has the same significance as transiting Mars inconjunct natal Saturn; however, it generally lasts for a longer period, indicating a sustained period of hardship and difficulties in the profession and work environment. This could involve unemployment or lack of work.

Transiting Mars Inconjunct Natal Uranus

This indicates a period of sudden, unexpected difficulties in work, health, business, joint money, corporate affairs, and mechanical and electronic systems. Unexpected problems could arise regarding friends, groups, and organizations. Unexpected problems could make the individual irritable and prone to sudden outbursts of anger.

Caution must be exercised in the use of machinery, electricity, explosives, dangerous chemicals, and fire if sudden accidents are to be avoided.

At this time, the individual can experience strong sexual desires that can also be a source of unexpected problems and irritations. Sudden, unexpected health and work difficulties can arise during this period.

When considering the departing Virgo-sixth house type of inconjunct, the individual should be safety-conscious at work. This is not the best time to experiment with new methods of doing things.

When considering the approaching Scorpio-eighth house type of inconjunct, conflicts are likely to arise over financial and sexual issues. Friendships are apt to become strained over failure or inability to properly handle financial affairs.

Transiting Uranus inconjunct natal Mars has the same significance as transiting Mars inconjunct natal Uranus; however, it is of longer duration, indicating a sustained period of disruptive and dangerous conditions in the individual's work and financial affairs. The individual needs to avoid impulsiveness and impatience in order to minimize these dangers.

Transiting Mars Inconjunct Natal Neptune

This indicates a period of emotional problems and confusing conditions. The individual will find it difficult to define and fully understand his or her desires, and thus be inclined to ineffectual action; this can be the result of conflicting subconscious desires and motives. There is potential for infectious diseases of a subtle and difficult-to-diagnose nature, and there could be danger of deception in matters of work, finance, or business. Emotional frustrations could lead to ill-conceived or confused action, and there could be an element of secrecy and intrigue involved in the individual's work, personal matters, and financial dealings. Subtle, but nonetheless dangerous, health hazards could be present in the working environment. This is a poor time to undergo surgery or anaesthesia or to take narcotic drugs. Sexual involvement could lead to infections and health problems. The individual could also be subject to disturbing psychic impressions.

When considering the departing, Virgo-sixth house type of inconjunct, caution is needed in regard to hidden dangers in the work environment that can adversely affect the health. These circumstances could also contain an element of deceit and secrecy, or one could be unaware of what is actually going on.

When considering the approaching, Scorpio-eighth house type of inconjunct, there is danger of confusion, intrigue, or deception involving business and financial affairs. This is a poor time for experimenting with psychic or occult matters. The individual could learn of a death involving mysterious circumstances.

Transiting Neptune inconjunct natal Mars has the same significance as transiting Mars inconjunct natal Neptune; however, it lasts for a much longer period of time, indicating a sustained period of confusing desires and impulses.

Transiting Mars Inconjunct Natal Pluto

This indicates a period of struggle and strenuous exertion and, in extreme cases, potential for serious danger affecting the individual's work, health, business, and professional affairs. The individual should avoid imposing his or her will on those in the working environment, and should not allow others to coerce him or her. Caution should be used in the working environment or in military or police situations. The individual may make power plays or be subjected to them in matters related to joint money, corporate business, insurance, taxes, or divorce-related financial matters. This is a poor time to handle financial dealings involving corporate money or joint resources.

Strong sexual desires are likely to arise at this time, which may be difficult to deal with in terms of their emotional and health implications. Any attempt to use occult methods to manipulate others is likely to have dangerous consequences at this time.

This is a dangerous period in terms of physical accidents, conflict, and injury. Any connection with dishonest or corrupt dealings could have especially dangerous consequences at this time.

When considering the departing Virgo-sixth house type of inconjunct, dangers arising from work or health situations are likely to be of primary importance. There will be a need for improved methodologies in business and work areas.

When considering the approaching Scorpio-eighth house type of inconjunct, remember that this is potentially a dangerous transit situation that could threaten important business dealings, even life itself, and should be handled with utmost care. Selfish motivation on the individual's part could lead to dangerous circumstances.

Transiting Pluto inconjunct natal Mars has the same significance as transiting Mars inconjunct natal Pluto; however, it is of much longer duration, indicating a sustained period of struggle and difficulty related to work, professional, financial, business, military, or police affairs. This is not a favorable time to initiate new projects or major changes.

18

Transits of Jupiter

Transiting Jupiter Inconjunct Natal Sun
See Transiting Sun Inconjunct Natal Jupiter.

Transiting Jupiter Inconjunct Natal Moon
See Transiting Moon Inconjunct Natal Jupiter.

Transiting Jupiter Inconjunct Natal Mercury
See Transiting Mercury Inconjunct Natal Jupiter.

Transit Jupiter Inconjunct Natal Venus
See Transiting Venus Inconjunct Natal Jupiter.

Transiting Jupiter Inconjunct Natal Mars
See Transiting Mars Inconjunct Natal Jupiter.

Transiting Jupiter Inconjunct Natal Jupiter
This indicates a period during which the individual may experience difficulties and a need for readjustment in matters related to higher education, legal affairs, long journeys, foreigners, and commerce involving faraway places. There could be a need to readjust the thinking patterns where religion and moral issues are con-

cerned. This is not a favorable time for taking risks or making expansive moves. There is a tendency to overlook important details, or there may be unexpected contingencies that make one's plans and commitments more costly than anticipated. Annoying domestic situations are likely to surface at this time; this could be the result of a tendency to take too much for granted where domestic affairs are concerned. This is an unfavorable period for dealing with hospitals, churches, universities, or other cultural institutions.

It is important to use good judgment and discrimination when bestowing favors as misplaced sympathies or wrong motives could cause problems.

When considering the departing Virgo-sixth house type of inconjunct, overindulgence of various kinds can result in health problems and interference in work.

When considering the approaching Scorpio-eighth house type of inconjunct, the individual should avoid over-expansion in business and financial affairs, and any tendency to force personal moral standards or judgments on others.

Transiting Jupiter Inconjunct Natal Saturn

This indicates a period of difficulties in legal, professional, and political affairs. This is not a favorable time for changing jobs, seeking employment or dealing with established people in positions of power and authority. Red tape, government regulations, legal difficulties, taxes, and problems with insurance, inheritance, divorce-related finances, or corporate money could interfere with the individual's work and profession. It is a poor time for business expansion or making important professional decisions. Dealings in long-distance commerce or legal affairs or with cultural institutions, foreign countries or people from faraway places are likely to have flaws that make them less than satisfactory. In general it is a time to take care of business as usual until a more favorable time arrives for making important decisions or moves.

When considering the departing Virgo-sixth house type of inconjunct, the individual is likely to be confronted with work and health problems resulting from professional, legal, or business aggravations.

When considering the approaching Scorpio-eighth house type of inconjunct, problems are likely to arise over taxes, insurance, inheritance, joint money, corporate money, child support, or spousal maintenance. The necessity could also arise to develop ecologically sound methods in business.

Transiting Saturn inconjunct natal Jupiter has the same significance as transiting Jupiter inconjunct natal Saturn; however, it is usually of longer duration, indicating a sustained period of burdensome, difficult-to-handle responsibilities.

Transiting Jupiter Inconjunct Natal Uranus

This indicates a period during which extravagance and waste can lead to unexpected difficulties. If the individual overextends or commits to more than he or she can adequately handle, unexpected detailed factors can cause a breakdown in work, business, financial, or corporate affairs. One should carefully examine the well-meaning but often impractical advice of friends, as at this time these overtures could have insincere, ulterior motives behind them. There is a tendency to ignore the practical realities necessary to achieve what the mind envisions.

Unexpected events can cause difficulties in the family or home environment; these difficulties are often related to the health of family members. There can also be a tendency to financially over-extend oneself to friends, groups, and organizations. The individual or his or her friends could entertain impractical religious, cultural, or educational ideas. In general, a sense of balance and practicality is needed at this time.

When considering the departing Virgo-sixth house type of inconjunct, problems related to work and health are likely to result from the individual's poor judgment, extravagance, and impracticality.

When considering the approaching Scorpio-eighth house type of inconjunct, extravagance and poor judgment will cause problems related to matters involving taxes, insurance, joint finances, corporate money, and divorce-related financial matters. Difficulties could arise over religious, cultural, educational, and moral ideas, friendships, and group associations. These are often related to money and financial dealings in some way.

Transiting Uranus inconjunct natal Jupiter has the same significance as transiting Jupiter inconjunct natal Uranus; however, it lasts for a longer period of time, indicating a sustained period of unexpected upsets in business affairs and the necessity for reevaluating one's ethical, cultural, educational, and moral viewpoints.

Transiting Jupiter Inconjunct Natal Neptune

This indicates a period of unrealistic, euphoric emotional attitudes that ultimately have unpleasant consequences for the individual's work, health, and finances. Often the individual entertains false notions that a cult, guru, or get-rich-quick scheme will solve all problems without much effort on his or her part. Such delusions and wishful thinking usually end in disappointment when the bubble bursts and reality makes itself felt.

The individual may seek to avoid work through escapist tendencies and involvement in alcohol, drugs, cults, or questionable religious practices.

When considering the departing Virgo-sixth house type of inconjunct, the individual's escapist tendencies could lead to health and work problems of various types. A tendency toward wool-gathering could cause inefficiency in work.

When considering the approaching Scorpio-eighth house type of inconjunct, the individual can suffer from self-deception about business, financial, or occult matters. He or she could also entertain unrealistic notions about the motivations and values of others.

Transiting Neptune inconjunct natal Jupiter has the same significance as transiting Jupiter inconjunct natal Neptune; however, it lasts much longer, indicating a sustained period for danger of self-deception and escapism involving work, health, and business.

Transiting Jupiter Inconjunct Natal Pluto

This indicates a period of difficulties in business, financial, ethical, and spiritual issues. The individual should exercise discrimination and sound judgment in attempting to improve or alter conditions regarding these matters; avoid grandiose desires for power, prestige, and wealth; and be cautious when dealing with those who have similar tendencies. There is also the danger of involvement in legal difficulties that pertain to business, insurance, taxes, inheritance, child support, and spousal maintenance.

Involvement in the occult or mystical practices should be carefully examined as to intent and purpose; otherwise, it would be very detrimental at this time.

When considering the departing Virgo-sixth house type of inconjunct, difficulties related to health, work, and ecological conditions in the working environment can become evident.

When considering the approaching, Scorpio-eighth house type of inconjunct, problems are generally related to insurance, joint money, corporate money, taxes, divorce-related finances, or misuse of occult powers. Legal entanglements are also likely to arise at this time.

Transiting Pluto inconjunct natal Jupiter has the same significance as transiting Jupiter inconjunct natal Pluto; however, it is of much longer duration, indicating a sustained period of entanglement in difficult financial, legal, ethical, and spiritual problems.

19

Transits of Saturn

Transiting Saturn Inconjunct Natal Sun

See Transiting Sun Inconjunct Natal Saturn.

Transiting Saturn Inconjunct Natal Moon

See Transiting Moon Inconjunct Natal Saturn.

Transiting Saturn Inconjunct Natal Mercury

See Transiting Mercury Inconjunct Natal Saturn.

Transiting Saturn Inconjunct Natal Venus

See Transiting Venus Inconjunct Natal Saturn.

Transiting Saturn Inconjunct Natal Mars

See Transiting Mars Inconjunct Natal Saturn.

Transiting Saturn Inconjunct Natal Jupiter

See Transiting Jupiter Inconjunct Natal Saturn.

Transiting Saturn Inconjunct Natal Saturn

This indicates a period of hard work, frustration, difficulty, and limitation in professional, business and work-related matters. This is an unfavorable time to change jobs, seek employment, or have important dealings with people in established positions of power and authority. Overwork can lead to exhaustion and lowered vitality with consequent health problems.

Problems can arise in partnerships or because of an inability to fulfill legal or financial commitments. Government restrictions and red tape are apt to interfere with the individual's professional affairs. The individual may also be called upon to care for an older or ailing person.

When considering the departing Virgo-sixth house type of inconjunct, unemployment, overwork, health problems, and conditions of servitude are likely to be a source of difficulty.

When considering the approaching Scorpio-eighth house type of inconjunct, burdensome financial responsibilities, restrictions, and problems related to joint money, corporate money, divorce-related finances, taxes, or insurance could be a source of worry.

Transiting Saturn Inconjunct Natal Uranus

This indicates a period of unexpected difficulties and setbacks related to insurance, taxes,

inheritance, financial and legal obligations, corporate money, technological innovations, and technology related to businesses and professional activities.

Burdensome responsibilities can arise involving friends, groups, and organizations. Friendships or group associations may even be based on ulterior motives, which could result in a sudden breakdown of the relationship.

Difficult responsibilities can arise that involve the care of health problems of older people or friends. This is a poor time to approach people of established power and authority with new ideas; in general, it is best to maintain the status quo until a more favorable time.

When considering the departing Virgo-sixth house type of inconjunct, the individual should avoid work situations that could be injurious to health and seek balance and moderation in handling important professional and work-related affairs. The individual could be subject to sudden disruptions in work because of illness or more other health problems.

When considering the approaching Scorpio-eighth house type of inconjunct, sudden problems and difficulties are apt to arise that involve joint money, corporate money, divorce-related finances, insurance, inheritance, or taxes.

Transiting Uranus inconjunct natal Saturn has the same significance as transiting Saturn inconjunct natal Uranus; however, it is of longer duration, indicating a sustained period of unexpected setbacks and difficulties related to financial, business, professional, and work-related affairs. Such difficulties often result from large-scale economic, political, social, and cultural forces beyond the individual's control.

Transiting Saturn Inconjunct Natal Neptune

This indicates a period of difficult and hard-to-diagnose work and health problems. The individual must guard against deceptive practices in work, medical, legal, and professional affairs, as well as in business dealings with hospitals, universities, and other institutions.

Some individuals will experience mental illness or hypochondria as a means of escaping burdensome practical work responsibilities. Hidden factors are likely to interfere with the individual's health and work. It is also a poor time to get involved in business and political schemes and intrigues. There is a tendency for emotional depression due to an unconscious stimulation of the memory of unpleasant past experiences.

In extreme cases, and if the natal horoscope shows similar tendencies, this period could result in institutionalization.

The individual may have the burden of secrecy in professional affairs under this transit, and also to bothersome skin, bone, or teeth problems. Or, they may have responsibility for caring for a family member or older person. This could interfere with work, health, and family.

When considering the departing Virgo-sixth house type of inconjunct, psychosomatic tendencies or other chronic physical and psychological health problems can interfere with the individual's work. Subtle factors in the working environment, such as toxic chemicals, could also endanger the individual's health. This is an unfavorable time for important dealings with older people in established positions of power and authority.

When considering the approaching Scorpio-eighth house type of inconjunct, the individual should avoid getting involved in business, corporate, or financial schemes and intrigues. Difficulties in legal and professional matters related to insurance, taxes, child support, spousal maintenance, and joint money are possible at this time. It is a poor time to experiment with psychic or occult practices.

Transiting Neptune inconjunct natal Saturn has the same significance as transiting Saturn inconjunct natal Neptune; however, it lasts for a longer period of time, indicating a sustained period of subconscious psychological difficulties and deceptive conditions in business and professional affairs.

Transiting Saturn Inconjunct Natal Pluto

This indicates a period of serious problems and difficulties involving professional matters, joint money, corporate business, technology, ecological issues, and dangerous intrigues, as well as serious occupational health hazards.

The manner in which these problems are handled can have important and far-reaching consequences. Utmost caution is needed when making legal commitments involving business, professional, and governmental affairs. In extreme cases, the individual may become involved in life-and-death issues. Serious matters can arise that involve friends, groups, and organizations. Any financial dealings that suggest criminal or underworld connections are best left strictly alone. The individual could become involved in power struggles with forces of good and evil that often relate to important matters of far-reaching consequence.

This is not a favorable time for involvement in psychic or occult practices because the individual can become open to destructive or evil forces.

When considering the Virgo-sixth house type of inconjunct, the individual can be exposed to serious health problems in the occupation; or, it may be necessary to completely reorganize or restructure occupational methods and activities. In extreme cases, serious health problems can arise that threaten the individual's life.

When considering the approaching Scorpio-eighth house type of inconjunct, old political, professional, and economic conditions on which the individual depends could be terminated or drastically changed. There could be the termination of old conditions and the initiation of new ones. The individual may have to deal with important and difficult matters related to professional finances and could become involved in important business or political power struggles that would present many annoying problems. The individual's work could in some way become involved with corporate or governmental secrecy and advanced technology.

Transiting Pluto inconjunct natal Saturn has the same significance as transiting Saturn inconjunct natal Pluto; however, it is of longer duration, indicating a sustained period of dealing with critical financial, political, ecological, technological, or occult issues of far-reaching consequence.

20

Transits of Uranus

Transiting Uranus Inconjunct the Natal Sun
See Transiting Sun Inconjunct Natal Uranus.

Transiting Uranus Inconjunct the Natal Moon
See Transiting Moon Inconjunct Natal Uranus.

Transiting Uranus Inconjunct Natal Mercury
See Transiting Mercury Inconjunct Natal Uranus.

Transiting Uranus Inconjunct Natal Venus
See Transiting Venus Inconjunct Natal Uranus.

Transiting Uranus Inconjunct Natal Mars
See Transiting Mars Inconjunct Natal Uranus.

Transiting Uranus Inconjunct Natal Jupiter
See Transiting Jupiter Inconjunct Natal Uranus.

Transiting Uranus Inconjunct Natal Saturn
See Transiting Saturn Inconjunct Natal Uranus.

Transiting Uranus Inconjunct Natal Uranus

This indicates a period of change and readjustment in the individual's friendships, group associations, creative projects, goals and objectives, and business affairs, especially those related to technology, humanitarian issues, or occult-related subjects.

Unpredictable circumstances beyond the individual's personal control are likely to force him or her to make sudden changes in his goals and objectives and the methods of realizing them.

Health problems related to nervousness or circulation could become evident at this time; these problems could involve the ankles or calves. The individual could hear of the sudden death of a friend or a radical alteration in the life of a friend.

When considering the departing Virgo-sixth house type of inconjunct, unexpected circumstances and difficulties can arise affecting the individual's health and work environment.

When considering the approaching Scorpio-eighth house type of inconjunct, unexpected problems and difficulties can arise relate to insurance, taxes, inheritance, joint money, spousal maintenance, or child support; this could include occult activity.

Transiting Uranus Inconjunct Natal Neptune

This indicates a period of sudden psychological difficulties affecting the individual or his or her friends through the stimulation of subconscious memories; or, this could come about through large-scale political, economic, ecological, or cultural forces beyond the individual's control. Some may become involved in mystical cults or off-beat groups that may be more of a liability than an asset. The individual's friends or group associates are likely to experience peculiar and disruptive circumstances in their lives that can indirectly create problems.

There is a tendency to become restless and dissatisfied with old conditions, especially those involving business and work.

Unexpected disruptive circumstances could affect the individual's home, or friends could create upsetting conditions on the domestic front.

The individual may also make important readjustments in religious, humanitarian, occult, and philosophic ideas, beliefs, and practices. Great caution should be exercised with anaesthesia and other drugs.

Some individuals may be subject to peculiar and disturbing psychic experiences at this time. This is a poor time to experiment with potentially dangerous drugs or psychic practices.

When considering the departing Virgo-sixth house type of inconjunct, the individual should avoid involvement in activities and practices that could endanger health or job stability.

Psychosomatic tendencies or psychological problems of the individual or friends could interfere with work efficiency.

When considering the approaching Scorpio-eighth house type of inconjunct, peculiar and mysterious circumstances can arise that involve business, higher education, and matters related to government funding, insurance, taxes, child support, spousal maintenance, inheritance, and corporate interests.

Transiting Neptune inconjunct natal Uranus has the same significance as transiting Uranus inconjunct natal Neptune; both transits last off and on for a year or longer.

Transiting Uranus Inconjunct Natal Pluto

This indicates a period during which sudden and unexpected cultural, ecological, political and economic changes or disruptions beyond the individual's personal control can force a drastic alteration in the lifestyle. Friendships, group affiliations, goals and objectives, and financial involvement with others, including corporate interests, are all subject to sudden and irrevocable change.

The individual could be subject to peculiar psychic experiences that could be disturbing, and even motivate lifestyle changes.

This is not a time to make important changes involving joint money, technology, insurance, taxes, inheritance, and the handling of collective resources.

This is not a favorable period for dealing with hospitals or institutions unless it is absolutely necessary.

When considering the departing, Virgo-sixth house type of inconjunct, unexpected circumstances can alter the individual's working conditions or affect the health. The individual could be subjected to work-related ecological hazards or working conditions that affect the nerves. Disruptive conditions could affect friendships or organizational associations.

When considering the approaching Scorpio-eighth house type of inconjunct, the individual is subject to unexpected dangers to life, financial investments, and fulfillment of goals and objectives. Forces beyond the individual's control could alter his or her destiny. In extreme cases, the individual or his or her friends could be in danger of their lives or entertain unwise ideas and goals. Drastic setbacks could occur involving corporate or financial interests and endeavors.

Transiting Pluto inconjunct natal Uranus has the same significance as transiting Uranus inconjunct natal Pluto; both transits last off and on for a year or longer, indicating a sustained period of major upheavals in the life of the individual.

21

Transits of Neptune

Transiting Neptune Inconjunct Natal Sun
See Transiting Sun Inconjunct Natal Neptune.

Transiting Neptune Inconjunct Natal Moon
See Transiting Moon Inconjunct Natal Neptune.

Transiting Neptune Inconjunct Natal Mercury
See Transiting Mercury Inconjunct Natal Neptune.

Transiting Neptune Inconjunct Natal Venus
See Transiting Venus Inconjunct Natal Neptune.

Transiting Neptune Inconjunct Natal Mars
See Transiting Mars Inconjunct Natal Neptune.

Transiting Neptune Inconjunct Natal Jupiter
See Transiting Jupiter Inconjunct Natal Neptune.

Transiting Neptune Inconjunct Natal Saturn
See Transiting Saturn Inconjunct Natal Neptune.

Transiting Neptune Inconjunct Natal Uranus

See Transiting Uranus Inconjunct Natal Neptune.

Transit Neptune Inconjunct Natal Neptune

This indicates a period of emotional and psychological confusion affecting the individual's health and ability to work, often resulting from the stimulation of unpleasant subconscious memories. The individual could display psychosomatic tendencies or be subject to peculiar illnesses that are difficult to diagnose. Also important during this transit is to guard against self-deception or deception by others in business or financial affairs. This is not a good period for indiscriminate psychic experimentation; neither is it a good period to deal with hospitals, universities, or other institutions. Because this transit can occur only in the latter part of life, the individual may go through difficult psychological or spiritual adjustments in preparation for the ultimate change called death.

The individual's health could be endangered by toxic chemicals, impure water, leaking gases, medication, or other subtle dangers.

When considering the departing Virgo-sixth house type of inconjunct, the individual's health and ability to handle daily activities could be affected. Hospitalization at this time is not advisable unless absolutely necessary.

The approaching Scorpio-eighth house type of inconjunct of Neptune to its own natal position does not occur in an average lifetime.

Transiting Neptune Inconjunct Natal Pluto

This indicates a period of subtle and irrevocable change in the individual's life involving business, finances, ecological issues, spiritual and psychological outlook, and the cultural context in which the individual functions. Such changes are often brought about by political, economic, and ecological forces beyond his or her control. The individual may be subject to strange, disturbing psychic experiences; hence, this is not a time to experiment with potentially dangerous psychic practices. The individual could be tempted to psychologically coerce others, or might be subjected to such treatment. This could affect the health, work, and financial status. The individual should guard against deception in financial and corporate affairs. There could also be concern about ecological and cultural concerns affecting the individual, or he or she could become involved in scientific or government secrecy.

When considering the departing Virgo-sixth house type of inconjunct, the individual can be subjected to subtle factors that can affect the health and ability to work. Subtle factors and details that escape notice can force the individual to improve or rework methodologies. There could even be subtle, but nonetheless deadly, occupational hazards, such as radioactivity or chemical poisoning. Great care and caution should be taken when administering drugs to one experiencing this transit.

When considering the approaching Scorpio-eighth house type of inconjunct, the individual can be subject to subtle intrigues involving business, corporate money, joint money, child support, spousal maintenance, insurance, taxes, or inheritance. During this period, the individual could develop an interest in the occult, although caution should be exercised in this area. Ecological matters and large-scale transformations are likely to concern the individual and be instrumental in changing his or her lifestyle.

Transiting Pluto inconjunct natal Neptune has the same significance as transiting Neptune inconjunct natal Pluto; both transits last off and on for a year or longer, indicating a sustained period of cultural, financial, work-related transformation, psychically subtle and inexorable, for better or worse. The individual could develop an interest in spiritual healing or new technological methods of healing.

22

Transits of Pluto

Transiting Pluto Inconjunct Natal Sun
See Transiting Sun Inconjunct Natal Pluto.

Transiting Pluto Inconjunct Natal Moon
See Transiting Moon Inconjunct Natal Pluto.

Transiting Pluto Inconjunct Natal Mercury
See Transiting Mercury Inconjunct Natal Pluto.

Transiting Pluto Inconjunct Natal Venus
See Transiting Venus Inconjunct Natal Pluto.

Transiting Pluto Inconjunct Natal Mars
See Transiting Mars Inconjunct Natal Pluto.

Transiting Pluto Inconjunct Natal Jupiter
See Transiting Jupiter Inconjunct Natal Pluto.

Transiting Pluto Inconjunct Natal Saturn
See Transiting Saturn Inconjunct Natal Pluto.

Transiting Pluto Inconjunct Natal Uranus

See "Transiting Uranus Inconjunct Natal Pluto.

Transiting Pluto Inconjunct Natal Neptune

See Transiting Neptune Inconjunct Natal Pluto.

Transiting Pluto Inconjunct Natal Pluto

This transit does not occur in an average life span.

Appendix I

Approaching Aspects: Approaching aspects are formed when the faster-moving planet (or luminary), having contacted the opposition to the slower-moving planet (or luminary), is moving toward the conjunction to that same planet.

Departing Aspects: Departing aspects are formed when the faster-moving planet (or luminary), having contacted the conjunction to the slower-moving planet (or luminary), is moving toward the opposition to that same planet.

Applying Aspects: Applying aspects are f6rmed when the faster-moving planet (or luminary) nears exact aspect to the slower-moving planet (or luminary), moving toward that contact.

Separating Aspects: Separating aspects are formed when the faster-moving planet (or luminary) diverges from the exact aspect to the slower-moving planet (or luminary), moving away from that contact.

Departing Semisextile: Taurus/second house-Venus/Moon—acquiring resources.

Approaching Semisextile: Pisces/twelfth house-Jupiter-Neptune /Venus—using resources of the subconscious mind and intuition.

Departing Sextile: Gemini/third house-Mercury—curiosity, thought, communication. Approaching Sextile: Aquarius/eleventh house-Saturn-Uranus /Mercury—intuitive ideas, friends, groups.

Departing Square: Cancer/fourth house-Moon/Jupiter-Neptune —need to overcome past conditioning and emotional problems.

Approaching Square: Capricorn/tenth house-Saturn/Mars—hard work to achieve ambitions; need for discipline, structure, and organization.

Departing Trine: Leo/fifth house-Sun/Pluto—creative self-expression, enjoyment, personal charisma, vitality.

Approaching Trine: Sagittarius/ninth house-Jupiter-Neptune—inspirational; expansive; intuitive guidance; benefits of religion, philosophy, cultural enrichment, higher education, and travel.

Departing Inconjunct: Virgo/sixth house-Mercury—need for efficient and practical approach; hard work; service; efficient methodology; practical thinking.

Approaching Inconjunct: Scorpio/eighth house-Mars-Pluto/Uranus—need to accept the inevitable; change; need to regenerate motives can bring occult and scientific understanding; transformative death of old attitudes and conditions.

Lightning Source UK Ltd.
Milton Keynes UK
UKHW011530240120
357556UK00001B/92